KARSTEN MASSEI, studied political scienc decided to train as a ₎ in Switzerland. Since then he has taught in a special needs day-school in Zurich, where he also lives. Besides this work, Karsten Massei gives courses and seminars on the practice of supersensible perception, spiritual enquiries into bees, and on the nature of animals, trees and medicinal plants. He also increasingly studies pedagogical themes.

CONNECTING WITH NATURE

*Earth and Humanity
—What Unites Us?*

Karsten Massei

Translated by Matthew Barton

TEMPLE LODGE

Temple Lodge Publishing Ltd.
Hillside House, The Square
Forest Row, RH18 5ES

www.templelodge.com

Published by Temple Lodge 2022

Originally published in German under the title *Erde und Mensch: Was uns verbindet* by Futurum Verlag, Basel, Switzerland, 2018

© Futurum Verlag, Basel 2018
This translation © Temple Lodge Publishing 2022

A CIP catalogue record for this book is available from the British Library

ISBN 978 1 912230 98 3

Cover by Morgan Creative
Typeset by Symbiosys Technologies, Visakhapatnam, India
Printed and bound by 4Edge Ltd., Essex

Contents

1
The names

With every name we utter, we enter a distinct and unique world. When we say: chair, tree, sea, boat, fish, we already come very close to what is meant by this name, for reality is hidden in it. Speaking it can mean being closer to the being or reality referred to than when we look at it, hold it in our hands or otherwise engage with it. When I speak a name or an idea, I enter into a tangible relationship with the being or reality this name or idea designates. This relationship is of a purely spiritual and soul nature and is unavailable to sense perception. Only a perception informed by purely soul or spiritual processes will enable me to consciously experience this relationship.

To gain experiences of this kind shows that the human soul possesses a supersensible nature. Besides the sensory plane there are further levels connecting the soul with the earth and her reality. The ordinary senses are not our only ones. We have others, but these require us to acknowledge that we can think above and beyond the sense world. Limiting our thinking to the sense realm means denying the foundations of our higher nature and thus depriving ourselves of essential experiences.

*

We possess inner senses which apprehend the names of beings as experiences that are hard to describe in words. To begin with, perhaps, they convey only very faint and delicate impressions which we must first learn to discern as such. It may be that we do not perceive them consciously at all to start with, since we are as yet too unfamiliar with them. We need patience in learning the language of the inner senses, as we do in learning any new language.

The human soul is a receptive, very sensitive entity. Nothing passes it by unnoticed. It has the gift of opening to everything that occurs around it. Everything—but truly everything—makes an impression on it: everything we experience, perceive, all images, all nuances of tone and shades of colour. All this falls upon the soul and leaves its trace; all is absorbed. Even if all that in this way gathers and accumulates in the soul in the course of a lifetime is largely inaccessible to the conscious mind, this does not mean it is absent from the soul.

*

The human soul has its own language: inklings, unexpected insights, certainties, intuitions. Often these are inexplicable but are due to the fact that we not only live in the sense realm but in others as well. To master this language we must use special terms and concepts that scarcely belong to modern culture. At least, they are not taught in our schools and universities. We are not taught there how to develop capacities that allow us to engage consciously with supersensible experiences.

Learning the language of the soul becomes a central and important task for those who experience supersensible realities. This is to do with the fact that these supersensible realities themselves do not immediately furnish us with the concepts that would enable us to think through what we experience. Supersensible experiences are perceptions for which suitable concepts still need to be found. And each person has to form the necessary ideas and concepts themselves. This is not a disadvantage but an altogether healthy process. Those who meet with supersensible experiences must themselves create the ideas and concepts to grasp for themselves and others what they are experiencing. We will not get further without a conceptual framework, and this is a labour that should not be undervalued. It is of great worth for it compels us to compare the various perceptions we gain, and to systematize them to a certain degree.

*

To open ourselves to what lives in names and surpasses the merely sensory sphere is a journey that can only be made by each person themselves. It is an individual, not a communal path which brings us closer to the mysteries of existence. This does not mean we will not meet friends upon the way, but we will have to dispense with everything originating in communal contexts that ties us to certain ideas or ideals and subordinates us to these. The moment we submit to outward forms we lose the freedom of the spirit that is essential for us if we are to turn to the mysteries of existence out of the power of our own being. Freedom is a possession all too easily withdrawn from us again, one that we even deprive ourselves of when we submit to conceptual systems and ideas. Human freedom is bound up with the capacity to be our own measure, that is, only to accept with caution standards asserted from without. In practice we are still in the process of learning and acquiring the capacity to develop this measure of our own. While the instances when this succeeds may still be rare, they are all the more valuable.

*

How do I make myself independent of the views and judgements of others yet still attend to the message for me that these contain? How do I acquire freedom from the compulsion which the views of others exert upon me? This will work best if I develop a free relationship with myself. The first step here can be the desire to dispel every lie I harbour about myself. I undertake not to lie to myself any more, so that I can then respond in a more neutral way to the opinions of others. If I become more neutral toward myself I can be more neutral also toward others. To dispense with self-deception requires resolve. Usually I will need to renew this resolve frequently. If I decide to combat self-deception I enter into a kind of conversation with myself. I face myself and demand something of myself, at the same time observing what effect this resolve has. I observe how I respond to what happens and how I relate to myself after making this resolve. At all events, I develop a different relationship to myself.

To face one's own self-deceptions means observing oneself more keenly. This means that I become aware of the compulsions living in my own soul, to which I succumb: drives and desires, envy, fears, anger, rage, lust for power or acclaim. These involuntary stirrings have a strong influence on our own behaviour: they fetter us for we are often unable to ward them off. Though we would like to be free and self-determined, we succumb to them even if we know that we will regret this later. One way to free ourselves from these compulsions is to accept them. They belong to us like other qualities, capacities and attributes. Only when I address them in a positive way will I be able to discover what they are trying to tell me. Usually they are the expression of a lack, an unlived longing, a hidden pain, an experience that has remained unconscious. Only once I have accepted them will I be able to feel myself free in relationship to them. To try to conceal them from myself is a strategy that does not lead to any real solution. They lose their power over me as soon as I have learned to value them—in other words, have found access to their value, their meaning. They are, in fact questions that destiny is asking of me.

*

The name by which I am called is only an outward name. I am still journeying toward my true name. I am hidden behind this outward name. I may scarcely have any inkling of the sound of my real name. In the end we are all on a journey toward discovering who we are. We can sense that many new and surprising discoveries await us on this path. Indeed, we must want to be surprised by ourselves, for we are a very long way from what we will become. The name by which we are called is at any rate only a pointer to the person we actually are and will actually become. To think that we are the one others and we ourselves mean when we say our name would be to stop far too short.

I only become independent in so far as I gradually come to know my own hidden name. I do this less through the power of thinking and picturing than through that of listening. The path toward experiencing my own, great name leads through inner stillness, for the words and concepts do not yet (and may never) exist to encompass it. I become independent to the degree that I practise a form of listening that reaches beyond the ideas and concepts I form of myself. I discover my greater name only beyond the confines of what can be uttered. Using words does not enable me to reach where I truly exist, and where I seek to come.

2
The senses

We have embarked upon a very long journey, haven't we? Perhaps we have previously been in everything: in every bush, petal, bird-feather, every colour, every person, each water-drop, cry, every grain of sand, every gesture, all falling and rising, every onward journey, all flow and ebb, every leap and withdrawal, all resistance and opening, ripening and dying, every death. Or one day we will have been born and will have died with everything that exists. Then we will have passed through every possible gateway without the least effort. As the butterfly lets the breezes waft it we will have journeyed and will journey further without reaching any limits, will pass simply from one realm into the next.

*

We will only learn something about the secret life of things when we relinquish the idea that the sense realm presents an insuperable barrier to our quest for knowledge. Of course it is necessary for us to learn to use our senses and our reason but this does not have to mean that we deny our inner senses a part in discovering the truth. By trusting our outer senses alone we dig a ditch that runs right through us, really: we divide our inner from our outer being. Only where the soul becomes inward, where what is outside becomes interior, does its distinctive life really begin. The soul finds within itself the powers of knowledge. Insight, cognition, is an inner act of the soul. In outward, sensory life are found the signs and pointers, the seeds, from which inner life unfolds.

The reality that presents itself to the senses is not the whole. As we develop an inner life, we can discover that reality is not and cannot in fact only be outward. Without inner reality it would not manifest at all. Reality *always* has an inward, a soul dimension. The perceptions we have unfold a life in the soul which in no way distances them from truth. On the contrary, they become truer when they unite with the soul, when they are allowed to ally and join themselves with it. Their true being can only be inwardly discerned as their outward form can be discerned through the senses. Goethe describes this as follows:

> It is a pleasant undertaking to enquire into nature and into oneself at one and the same time, doing injury neither to nature nor to one's spirit but rather bringing each into balance with each through a mild and gentle interplay.[1]

*

In the soul lives a strong need to immerse itself in the light of other beings' existence, to dream its way into the inner reality of what presents itself outwardly to us. The soul seeks to perceive by sleeping into phenomena, though without relinquishing wakefulness either. Awakening in the light that lives in such manifold ways in all things and beings, the soul enters into the life of the earth. But these things and beings too wish to live in the human soul, wish to be felt and perceived by the human soul and spirit. It is indeed the beings themselves that we know in our environment that wish to unite with us, so as to touch into the mystery that the human being is for them. If we open ourselves to nature in all tranquillity, we can begin to hear this question from the beings around us: 'Who are you, O human being, who are more than all of us, a being possessing soul and spirit as your inward capacity? Do you know that your gift to us is the sacred substance of transformation?'

*

It is possible to develop intuitive observation of the earth and her beings. By doing this we enter into a close relationship with the earth: we truly integrate the phenomena, the beings, surrounding us—or in other words, we feel things and beings with our inner powers of soul. As the person we are, we enter into relationship with the earth and as a result the limits and hindrances vanish that make us feel separate from her. Our intellect is a key organ of perception, but so also is our heart, and serves to form judgements and gain insights. With the powers that live in our heart we understand things intuitively. Through them we raise the barriers that characterize the relationship of the intellect to reality. The heart 'knows' for powers stream from it that overcome all separation. It possesses a sense, really a sense of truth, through which it gains empathy with and discernment of the inner state of another being or living context, since it experiences it as its own. Through the heart what is outward becomes inward.

The powers of the heart can be dimmed. In these powers the whole of our being is always also contained, with all our aspects: *all* colours and shades of the soul live in the heart. If someone delves into the spiritual mysteries of the earth, therefore, they will also always discover themselves, their own soul-gold, their own luminosity, but also their shadows, their lower nature. We cannot overlook ourselves since, in the power of the heart, we ourselves are the *path* leading to the mysteries of the earth. At every stage of our path we encounter ourselves, also with our shadows, since the soul's capacity for perfidy, hatred and violence hinders our access to the secrets of the beings of the earth who repulse us.

Deep encounters with nature are therefore always also self-encounters, and thus a path to self-knowledge: we always make our way through everything as the person we have so far become. But from nature comes always a prompting to us not to remain as we are but to transform ourselves. To behold nature intuitively, thus through the heart's gifts of discernment, includes looking clearly and truthfully at ourselves.

3
Listening

One can experience how things and beings have fallen silent, that they are mute. It is as if they no longer reveal themselves directly to the observer—as if they had noticed that we no longer speak the same language as they do, as if they despised us. It sometimes seems as if they were conspiring against human beings, preferring instead to hide in wait. We can ask ourselves what has happened to the allure they must once have possessed, which in the past gave them an apparent affinity with humankind.

There are tales from early eras of humanity in which the commonality of human beings with the beings surrounding them shines out unmistakeably. In an Irish legend, Túan mac Cairill relates to the Irish monk Finnian how he has, over the course of a long life, transformed himself into all kinds of animals. He says this:

> I saw that I was hairy and tufty and bristled as a savage boar; that I was lean as a stripped bush; that I was greyer than a badger; withered and wrinkled like an empty sack; naked as a fish; wretched as a starving crow in winter; and on my fingers and toes there were great curving claws, so that I looked like nothing that was known, like nothing that was animal or divine. And I sat by the pool weeping my loneliness and wildness and my stern old age; and I could do no more than cry and lament between the earth and the sky, while the beasts that tracked me listened from

behind the trees, or crouched among bushes to stare at me from their drowsy covert.[2]

*

In the wonderful book Anam Cara *by John O'Donohue, the following words appear:*

> True listening brings us in touch even with that which is unsaid and unsayable. Sometimes the most important thresholds of mystery are places of silence. To be genuinely spiritual is to have great respect for the possibilities and presence of silence.[3]

Yes indeed, we are learners at the boundaries of spiritual space. We can enter this space if we adapt ourselves to its laws. We always do this when we listen attentively, when we allow another being, animal, plant but also a landscape or another person to speak their true nature to us. To connect with another being's reality is not just a matter of our alert senses but above all of our inner senses: offering the other being the open space it needs to impart itself.

Without human attentiveness, the beings of plants and animals, but also the elemental beings alive in the landscape, in lakes, rivers and mountains, feel a decisive lack. They dwindle because human beings withdraw from them the attention they need. From the soul can issue a power that blesses and enlivens, that addresses itself lovingly, appreciatively and sympathetically to the creatures and beings of the earth. Simply by virtue of existing we heal if we dispense the power of attention. This is a healing current that is easily underestimated because it is invisible and its effects cannot be measurably determined. But those who have some experience of this will confirm that surprising transformations can occur in a garden, a room, a house, a community or a living creature through loving attentiveness. This does not mean such attentiveness is enough. In many cases further steps will be needed, but this prepares a good soil.

Every observable detail is worth pondering attentively, for everything, every small matter, every little aspect, is always also a key to unlock the whole. This is inevitable. The moment our inner gesture of observation of, say, a leaf, a honeycomb, a scuttling ant, or the call of a bird is sustained by the loving power of devotion, we can suddenly, perhaps surprisingly, feel ourselves very close to the creature or entity in question, and this can give rise to insights we had no inkling of before.

*

It is possible to transpose ourselves into other beings' existence. In the same way that we naturally inhabit our own body, so, through the power of consciousness, we can also slip— or let us say 'wish ourselves'—into a different one.

It is possible to translate ourselves into a bee, a horse, a plant or a metal. In doing so we will gain experience of the forms of consciousness of the beings of the world outside us. We are surrounded by consciousness that is reflected in all the various visible life forms in which we participate on the earth. We can even transpose ourselves into our own inner organs and will discover this allows us to describe the liver, the kidneys or the larynx as forms of consciousness.

What surrounds us wants to speak to us. We easily misunderstand this language if we drown it out too much with our own speech. But we can seek to allow the gestures, colours and movements to enter us. We can enliven in ourselves the desire to slip into what lives in the world around us. We can awaken to the true mobility of our soul, which is able to slip into the delicate form of a plant, the activity of a bee, the urgent rush of a river, the up-soaring gesture of a mountain, the attentiveness of a horse or the soul life of another person.

A person who listens feels like a pupil who is being taught by these forms, colours, gestures and movements. He must not try to anticipate what kind of teaching he will receive. Let us forget our previous ideas, even our questions, for they all too easily hinder us when we appeal to them. By contrast we can trust in the beings that show us through their sensory form that they harbour within them more than this outward life alone—that they are pervaded by a life full of wisdom that acts entirely out of cosmic intelligence.

4
Elemental beings

We always stand at the threshold to the world of spirit, but this does not mean we are aware of it. We can only exist as human beings because the world of spirit acts directly within us at every moment. No organ function could otherwise be sustained; we could not take a single step, nor think a thought, let alone form a resolve. Our existence is founded on the fact that we are beings in whom the beings of the spiritual world unfold their activity. The living functions of our body, our soul capacities and our spiritual capacities depend upon us being deeply enmeshed with the world of spirit. Our existence at the threshold of worlds is a living truth that becomes experienced reality for those who awaken to their inner life. In especially clear moments we can discover that the power of our consciousness enables us to discern this threshold in full wakefulness. Then we feel and perceive that we are a threshold being, that the place where we truly stand is at the threshold of worlds. And then we know too that part of our task is to learn to stand there. We find also that this is no simple task. We will repeatedly be challenged and tested, and will need to invoke a great deal of attentiveness, care and devotion.

*

Upon this path we find support through the spirit beings of nature that live in every landscape, in gardens and forests, in great rivers and mountains, and in cities, for like us they stand wholly within the stream of time. The elemental beings safeguard the life of the earth, sustain it and bring it forth, which is why the stream of time also passes through their kingdom. They wish to tell us what they learn as their store of wisdom from the lofty beings of the spiritual world. They wish to tell us of the teachings they receive from the world of spirit. They wish to impart to us the lessons they continually receive when high angels appear before them and urge them to listen attentively since only in this way will they learn what they need to know to be able to accomplish their sacred work for the earth and humankind.

Deepening our observation of nature leads to us experiencing how our own soul emerges from the natural context: it is the inward face of externalized nature. Within the soul outward reality rises in so far as an inner world of perception forms there, a second, germinal Creation. The elemental beings speak of this, looking up to humankind because they experience us as a germinal being. They are created beings who do not themselves create—rather, the process of creation passes through them. They do not possess the spark of creativity inherent in the human soul. The ability to be an artist, thus to create out of one's own inner pictures, is entirely lacking in them. Entirely surrendered to the wisdom upon which the world's existence is founded, they can teach us but for the same reason are not beings who realize freedom.

*

We repeatedly hear from elemental beings that they are not primarily interested in being seen and perceived by human beings. What they wish, rather, is to see us. But we are very talented in making ourselves invisible to them. Our conduct is of a kind that makes us vanish from the gaze of nature beings. Thoughts that exclusively obey materialistic ideas conceal the thinker from them. The same is true of feelings and actions. But at the same time we have many opportunities to add spiritual substance to the earth's existence, something which makes us visible to beings of the elemental worlds. Only when they observe that someone turns lovingly and selflessly to them do they find it possible to appear before us. It is part of our human task to form an inner relationship with the world of a kind that enables the elemental beings to meet us. They can make next to nothing of all we do that sunders us from the earth. For them it is like a shadow we wrap around ourselves. They cannot penetrate it for it costs them too much effort. Only loving attention, thoughts that go deep, actions that respectfully acknowledge things and beings, enable nature beings to enter into a deep relationship with us.

*

We can hear this message from the elemental beings: the human being is the most wholesome and healing medicine for the earth. If we understood what this meant and made it into a principle of daily life, of civilization even, the face of the earth would be transformed. The earth hungers for a nourishment that can only arise when human beings really make use of their powers of soul and spirit. As yet people have no true knowledge of the degree to which their inner life affects the existence of the beings of the elemental world and thus of the earth. We are still in the process of acquiring this. With our powers of spirit and soul we create a centre that substantially helps shape the living world around us. Each of us can begin to gain such experiences. We must only be willing to shape and determine our own inner stance. A fundamental stance of positivity and affirmation exerts an influence on all around us that becomes immediately apparent. Affirming life is a power that multiplies unseen amongst the beings of the elemental world. Either sooner or later they will reward in their own way the person from whom this emanates, who will come to feel the tangible fruits of this inner attitude in their own life and destiny. For instance, new perspectives will dawn, new friendships, or entirely new inner impulses. The earth rewards the person who really stands up for her, even if this be simply through the power of affirming one's life and destiny.

*

The beings of the elemental world are very manifold and diverse. They enliven, breathe through and resonate through the whole earthly world. The whole tapestry of the sense world only becomes manifest because a countless number of invisible beings weave it tirelessly. Nothing perceptible upon the earth is without being. All sensory existence proceeds from the activity of beings who live in the elemental world. Elemental powers, elemental beings always participate in it. The elemental beings fulfil this task devotedly. We can see this devotion when we attend to the care, lawfulness and beauty of the physical world. It is thanks to the deeds of the elemental spirits that we humans find the physical life conditions we need. Those gifted with sight of the work of the elementals will be able to testify that the earth becomes manifest through the loving deeds of these beings.

The beings of the elemental world receive from higher beings of Creation the spiritual patterns or blueprints they use to produce, enliven and sustain the phenomena of the sense world. In this way they are the angels' labourers. The ideas of the angels are the patterns according to which they work. Their work involves filling with physical substance the spiritual forms the angels reveal to them. But we must conceive their work such that, in working in the service of higher powers, at the same time they become part of what they produce. They are spellbound within what they give rise to. Only when what they have made manifest passes away again, in other words wilts, rots or collapses, are they released from their state of enchantment.

*

A power proceeds from the human being that can bind, fetter and imprison the beings of the elemental world but also multiply, enrich and release them. When someone makes something like a component or even just elaborates a plan or diagram, they bind beings of the elemental world. When they destroy or dissolve something, they release them. But through our feelings and thoughts, too, we affect the elemental beings. As stated, it is of great importance for the elemental beings that we develop an awareness of the consequences of our thinking, feelings and actions for the elemental world. We can nourish or rob the beings that live in this world depending on how we relate both to our inner life and the life around us.

*

The destiny of human beings is bound up with the collaboration of beings of the elemental world. Their work creates the basis for us living out our destiny on earth. Ultimately their work serves humanity. Only through them do we find the physical world in which we can meet, fulfil and transform our destiny. Without the light of the sun, the wind, water, and also the solid earth upon which we make our way, an earthly destiny would be inconceivable. The elemental beings create the foundation for all experiences we have in our life on earth. They fashion the living context that continuously surrounds us and in which we fulfil our destiny.

However, the beings of the elemental world also have a deep relationship with the human being's faculties of soul and spirit. No intuition we have would be possible without the influence of the elemental beings. Nor could the alternation between sleeping and waking life happen without their activity. And in precisely the same way, birth and death cannot arise without their influence. In fact, every destined encounter only comes about because they unfold their protective activity.

5
Diverse elemental beings

At the threshold to the world of spirit stand three gateways, shining out toward the person who approaches them. Through them we can come into contact with various realms of the spiritual world, and behold how this spiritual world is connected with earthly phenomena. The ways in which the spirit world acts within the earthly realm are manifold: these gateways teach us about the three most fundamental ones. We can call them the gate of life, the gate of the soul and the gate of spirit. In them becomes visible the degree to which the actions of life, soul and spirit become active within terrestrial realities. By concerning ourselves with the world of elemental beings we look primarily through the gateway of life—though not exclusively for of course these beings also bear soul and spirit impulses into the existence of the earth. Our observations so far have shown that the beings of the elemental world are themselves threefold in nature, engaged not only with life forces but also mediating qualities of soul and spirit.

*

I want to introduce various beings from the elemental world so that readers can gain a sense of their ways of being and working. The first is the spirit of a river. I met him on a walking tour in the Swiss Alps. His being extends over part of a river that has collected on a high plain, and has just fallen into the valley through a steep gorge. The water was frothing in turbulent vigour. The spirit looked at me with astonishing calm. This calm was necessary to restrain the waters. He bore a crown on his head in which, as I beheld, stood beings, high mountain beings, whose servant he seemed to be. His work involved reconciling the numerous water spirits with the light beings who merged with the water here. Through the sunlight they streamed toward the water. The river spirit had a great deal to do to forge this union, needing first to calm and tame the water spirits, bring them to a degree of stillness so that this union could be accomplished. Through the form they assumed as they sprayed upward, the waterdrops were able to take up light. It can really be said that the tiny spirits in each of the countless waterdrops sucked light into the water. The light they received passed into the river as a nourishing strength. Thus a union was occurring here between two different kinds of beings, the miniscule waterdrop spirits and the light beings that sailed down to earth in the sunrays. The river spirit was creating the spiritual space within which this union could take place. Momentarily flying upward, the water droplets no longer belonged to the river but in a sense became independent beings with an openness to receive the light playing over the river, and able to conduct it back into the river as soon as they rejoined it.

What the river spirit does also has significance for human beings. Through his activity he makes a particular capacity available to us. The moment we die, our soul separates from the body and lives its way into the world of light, which the river spirit connects with the physical world. In the same way as the drops separate from the flowing river, so the soul separates from the body. The difference is that the droplets soon fall back into the river again while the human soul undergoes a longer separation from the body.

The activity of the river spirit cultivates the strength we need after death to leave the body behind us and to enter into a union with the world of spirit.

But there is another condition too in which we are surrendered to light during our lifetime: when we *think*—provided we do so in a way that allows us to receive intuitions. If we wish to be open to intuitions we must be able to open ourselves to the cosmic soul light that surrounds and envelops the earth. The powers we need for this are the same as those used by the river spirit when he creates the spiritual space in which light can unite with water.

*

An elemental being inhabits every leaf. It is born the moment the leaf emerges as a physical organ of a plant, something that occurs already in the leaf-bud. When the first indication of the leaf which is later to unfold becomes apparent, the leaf spirit has already been born, though to begin with he is bound up with the leaf in a state that we can term embryonic. When the leaf emerges the spirit too unfolds into his full existence: he fills out the leaf but his energy extends beyond the physical leaf. To the supersensible gaze the leaf spirit possesses a particular dynamic gesture that characterizes each plant species. Usually a specific relationship between watery, terrestrially-oriented and light-permeated processes comes to expression in this gestural dynamic.

It is difficult for the leaf spirit to make contact with the person who beholds him for he is to a high degree bound up with the plant's life processes, in fact held in enchantment there. He surrenders himself entirely to these processes. Through him the leaf acquires an inner, spiritual life through which it enables the plant to exist in the stream of life. As soon as the leaf ages, the leaf spirit starts to detach itself from it and becomes free. The physical world exhales him and he reunites with the being in the spiritual world from which he first emerged. This high being is the same as the power which holds the plant in safekeeping from the world of spirit. We can picture it as the life-stream which enables each separate plant on earth to be a living and developing entity.

*

In every landscape live a multiplicity of elemental beings, together creating the sum of a particular landscape or location. We can therefore call the elemental beings the guardians of landscape. They in turn are united under a high being, the angel of the landscape. From the angel of a landscape, a city, a particular place (such as a mountain, hill or lake) spiritual threads pass to every single being of the elemental world who all feel beholden to and united with the landscape angel. Seen in this way, every elemental being is always subject to the dominion of an angel of the landscape.

When visiting an island situated in a large Swiss lake, I became aware of this context. This island had once been an important site of pilgrimage. Pilgrims were ferried over from the shore then rested on the island or spent the night there before being ferried to the farther shore. On this island I encountered a lofty elemental being who still bore signs pointing to the island's former importance as a place of pilgrimage. From his chest hung a cloth that showed the face of Christ crowned with thorns. He had great, angel-like wings, the eye of God hung over him, and he held a golden chalice in his hands. He showed me that his tasks had once included care of the pilgrims who often arrived on the island tired and sick. But above and beyond this he was concerned with ennobling the human soul. I saw that he had attended the Masses that were celebrated on the island. This high being of the elemental world is embedded in a spiritual existence that is connected with landscape on the one hand but extends further, having the task of serving human evolution. This being missed the rituals that had once been celebrated on the island and experienced it as a blessing when we (my wife and I) offered him a short ritual. The attention we brought toward him was already an important event for him. He very much desired to find access to the realities of the modern era but was still bound up with what had taken place upon the island in earlier times. If we approach the island in such a way that we bring esteem for the task it once fulfilled but at the same time consider in thought and action the elemental beings who live there, who have helped sustain and support what happened there, these beings can gradually let go of their former role and seek out new ones.

*

At waterfalls we find important beings of the elemental world. They ascend the falls of plunging streams. Above a waterfall they unite in a high being who forms a transition between the elemental world and the world of the angelic hierarchies. If we sense this we can be seized by deep humility. We can discover that this high being helps nurture human evolution. He holds open the doorway that connects the world of unborn and dead souls with the earthly realm. We can perceive in this being something like a spiritual ladder upon which human souls ascend and descend. But here we also observe elemental and fairy beings who are involved in this process and accompany human souls as they are born and die.

*

During a trip with friends along the coast of Norway, I became aware of an elemental being, a fairy who sat upon a wall of undressed stones and wept. Only after a long while did she reveal the reason for her grief. It was here that she had lost the person whom she had accompanied through many incarnations when he set sail from this place. The wall on which she sat surrounded a grove of sandthorn bushes that stood fast in the fierce wind. She invited us there. She said her human had departed from his original goal, affiliating himself with powers that forbade her to follow him further. After a while she asked me whether I would be willing to help her. I hesitated, for I did not know what she wanted me to do. Finally I assured her I would do as she wished. This gave her hope—already my promise sufficed to free her from her pain. From that moment on she was released from her enchantment and in the following days, during which she accompanied us, disclosed to us some of her secrets. She was a body elemental being, such as we all possess, who was now on the search for new tasks.

*

Finally I want to speak of elemental beings who describe themselves as members of the fairy race. They are profoundly connected with human evolution. Deeply familiar with human spiritual evolution, they have manifold tasks. Thus they accompany individuals through their biography, supporting them in the development of their soul and spirit capacities. There are children who receive their influence from the very beginning of life, being inspired and taught by them. Someone who can sense the beings of the elemental world will be aware when a child is connected with and influenced by a fairy being. Children show this through the way they relate to others: they have great understanding of the individuality of other human beings, their needs and true tasks. Such children are continually involved in supporting the development of people in their surroundings, but naturally do this in the ways and with the means of a child. In many cases adults will need to handle these children very carefully and caringly and help them in the great tasks which they face. If they do not receive this support, they will encounter great hindrances in life.

Many children have contact with the beings of the fairy race, but lose it over time due to lack of understanding from the adult world. Yet it is always possible to regain this later in life. Encountering these wondrous beings is one of the most poignant experiences we can have of the elemental world. They are reticent, for above all they respect each person's freedom; but they willingly disclose their stores of wisdom to one able to attune to them. Part of their task involves revealing wisdoms that were safeguarded in the mysteries of earlier times to people today who are willing to receive them.

6

Messages from the elemental world

Here I would like to cite the words of an elemental being who calls himself the landscape king. He is a high being of the elemental world whom I encountered unexpectedly in a quiet wood in spring. Suddenly he stood there, a noble figure before me. He was only a little shorter than I, bore a crown and a reddish cloak interwoven with golden threads. Without much ado, he addressed the following words to me, which, since I fortunately had with me a pen and notebook, I was able to record:

> These words are addressed to you human beings: Hear, become hearers, hearkeners at the membranes of your soul. For it is there you will hear the truth, where you become inward, where you gain access to the mother of your soul, to the powers that bring you forth from within you. You exist there and have not yet fully gained yourselves. Those who seek their origins find themselves. And your origin is in the realm that we, the beings of the living earth, fill and pervade. We are the guardians of the spirit, of spirit worlds that have brought you forth. We stand at the threshold of your inner light, for it is the gateway to your spirit provenance. We stand where you look far too rarely. But out of the inner space, the secret space of your souls, shines a quintessential light. We behold the shining of your souls with far more clarity than you can as yet behold it. Each of you bears a quint-essential light in the foundations of your soul, which is the epitome of what you can give to the earth, to

the world, and through which the earth and the world can mature and develop.

We, as beings of the threshold, wish to serve you, to open for you a path to your soul's inner region. This is the Christmas path. We urge you to spend much time outside in the period of Christmas. Breathe the inner light, the intimate luminosity of nature at this time of year. It has a great affinity with the light that lives in your soul, with which you are in the process of becoming acquainted. You are our brothers and sisters because this soul light shines in the deep grounds of your being. Try to experience how you can become one with occurrences outside you by feeling the affinity between the secret light with which the world of elemental beings adorns itself in the Christmas period and the light that has shone at the bottom of your soul since primordial times. This inner light of the soul originates from the beginning, and only gradually have you become what you now are—beings who no longer experience their luminosity because outward shimmerings of the sense world are so bright and dazzling, and drown out the subtle inner sounds of the soul.

And you will find your inner light again when you come to us as hearkeners, as quiet, still receivers of the tranquil light, the Christmas light. In this season the world becomes inward, the beings of the elemental world turn toward what is happening within the earth, what is accomplished there. Amongst us is a beholding, a wonder, a gaze upon the interior of the earth, which you can experience. In the earth is an inner life of illumination. We behold it when we turn toward the earth during the Holy Nights. And we behold it in you.

O human beings, you are bearers of the inner light of the earth. You experience the Christmas of your soul, the rebirth of your soul existence when you truly seek your beginnings, your strength, within yourselves. Do not shy from looking into yourselves, for you do not encounter yourselves there, not your ordinary, daily selves, but rather you meet what your everyday being proceeds from. Who is that? you ask. How can we, as beings of the threshold, tell you? We only outwardly experience what lives inwardly in you as the true nature of your being.

When you turn toward yourselves as spirit seekers, you turn toward the earth, toward your sacred strata of life. This is how it appears to us, who guard for you the threshold between the realm of the visible and the realm of the invisible.

There we stand and live as a chorus of many-voiced, manifold, many-hued and richly configured beings, bringing forth the sensory appearance in which you live upon earth. Like you, we are entangled in earth existence. Only one being is still more entangled in earth existence, has succumbed wholly to it. This is the Lord of the Earth, of the solid earth, who has tormented the earth until it has become solid and fixed, stone-hard, almost irredeemable.

But he created your foundation. We are concerned for him, for he is betrayed and therefore becomes ever more inflexible and recalcitrant—for only a few understand that it is human beings who must create the spiritual foundations of renewal for this being who has furnished the substrate of sensory life. It is up to human beings to redress the spirit deeds of the earth's solidifier, by accepting and acting on the responsibility they have toward the earth.

A rebirth can occur at Christmas; the spirit being of the child can be born within earth existence if the human being acknowledges responsibility toward the earth. The renewal of the earth is not something that can be accomplished without the involvement of the human being. You participate decisively in this renewal by standing with your whole being in mysterious resonance with the earth, with its conditions and stratas. The solidifier of the earth, Ahriman, wishes to be as free as the human being has become free by virtue of the solid earth arising.

Through human beings, through their devoted love for the earth, the beings of the earth mature and evolve. As a mother devotedly cares for her child, so the earth should rest as devotedly in the soul's heart, in your soul inwardness. Then you are the earth's guardian, bearer of the earth's mission to transform what cannot itself embark upon transformation. For human beings to evolve into what they are, many other beings had to renounce their own evolution. In doing so they surrendered responsibility and the impulse for transformation to the human being. That is how it is, and it is important to grasp the real relationships existing between the beings of the earth.

*

The beings of the elemental world have wishes of humankind that come to expression in this verse I received while preparing for a journey:

The earth speaks,
every place expresses
what has been imprinted into it
from the other side,
from worlds of spirit.
Spirits want to speak to human beings.

Redemption is served
when these spirits
lie within a person's ear
since a world opens to them
which of themselves they do not know.

Hearken, human beings, to the sounds,
attend to the signs,
to the script of the earth;
it passes through you,
through your life,
through each of your perceptions,
through your deeds.

Thus speak the spirits
who ask you for redemption,
out of your high power
that lives in you by virtue of gods.

Transform what needs to be transformed,
out of the light of life
that glows in you since primal beginnings
and sustains you and the earth
who is your child
and also the mother
of your life.

Care for this wellspring,
your mother.
She lives from the child of love,
from every step you take
and that you refrain from.

Take this child with you.
It is the gift of the great world to you.

Do not let it wither,
for it wishes to live through you,
for it wishes to live in you,
for it wishes to live in the earth.

The treasure store of life of the great mother—
you bear it within you
as the sacred core of your being.

*

Now follow words showing what the elemental beings desire of humankind. I received them in a pass in the Swiss Alps:

Let go of what you
regard as life
your ideas
your wishes
only then can life's
felicity speak to you
the vitality of life—
we simply flow
through you
through your body
your will
your being
and flow through those
for whom you stand up
and are
and act
and surrender your life
lay it
in the Mother's womb
the Mother of life

swim once more
　in her life sap
　　in her amniotic liquor
　　　as you swam once when you came
　　　　to learn how to grow
　　　how to emerge from yourself
　　how to live with the earth
　be of good cheer
things will go well
　things are going ever better
　　things are already going well
　　　yes
　　　　yes
　　　　　yes

7
The lofty life of the trees

If we meet trees like old friends we will observe how mysterious they are. The longer we attend to them the more regard and respect we can feel for them. As soon as we devote ourselves to them patiently and intently, we are seized by a range of different feelings and sensations which seem unclassifiable to begin with. It is as if we are standing before beings who speak a language we do not know. This is the language of their hidden life, their diverse gestures of growth, their forms, rhythms and configurations. Truly, every tree is a wonderful gathering of the most varied gestures. We can ask how we can awaken these to utterance. In their shape and its mutability something essential is unmistakeably communicated: they speak to us! The language of trees is the language of their gestures. It might be objected that the same is true of all living phenomena. Every phenomenon can be seen as a gesture through which a being imparts itself. This is true. But in the case of trees the connection between their growth gestures and their hidden being can become strikingly apparent to the observer, for they reveal their intrinsic nature in forms of growth that survive, sometimes, for many hundreds of years. The permanence of their gestures makes it especially easy for us to experience and discern the connection between gesture and essential being. In this sense the trees instruct our capacities of discernment. Through them we can learn to read the phenomena of life. Those who seek to do so are invited to pass through the university of trees.

*

Those who carefully and repeatedly approach a big tree standing on its own will not fail to sense a significant encounter occurring. We feel received. Approaching the tree, we enter a full space, we experience a meeting with a being. What we feel here is the spirit of the tree who inhabits the visible shape of the tree. He does not become visible to the senses yet dwells in the tree for many decades or centuries.

It should be emphasized that it is really only through true regard, through a gaze of respect, that we acquire the right to encounter this inner being of spirit. There is indeed a threshold, a protected sphere before the world of spirit, which we can only enter if we give sufficient respect and attentiveness to sense phenomena. This is particularly true of tree spirits. They reveal themselves most to those who esteem their outward physical form. They have little to show those who fail to perceive them, considering their sensory form as inessential. Thus we can already invoke an encounter with the spirit of the tree if we consciously turn our thoughts to the sensory manifestation of the tree in question. Spirits are pleased to reveal the outward form of their life. They want to be seen; they love to be perceived by the human being. Tree spirits say of this: Your gaze and the touch of your hands caress us. By starting to live within you, a new life also begins in us.

*

We can have this surprising experience: that every tree, and indeed every single tree, stands in a distinct relationship to the individual human being. We can say that this relationship is one in which the single tree relates to the deeper essence of our being. A single tree does not speak to the spiritual archetype of the human being, as is true more of herbaceous plants, but it speaks to each individual person. We can actually feel that the tree which we approach or under which we sit, relates to our specific individuality. The unmistakeable feeling can arise that we are being observed. This is because the spirit of the tree is a lofty elemental being. Tree spirits are mighty beings of the elemental world.

*

Here I would like to describe an experience that drew my attention to the connection between tree spirits and wood. On one occasion I was on holiday with my family in northern Italy. Without knowing where I would end up, I set out on a walk one morning. I simply went wherever the elemental spirits led me. The path kept climbing until I had left the last houses of the town behind me. The trail ran alongside an overgrown meadow, where I became aware of a flowering hawthorn. Its crown was full of humming bees visiting the flowers. I was surprised and pleased to meet this tree here and observed it for a while. Right next to it I noticed an olive tree, a species particularly abundant in that region. I also saw an oak tree very near by. And I wondered about the encounter of these three trees. At this an elemental being appeared beside me, a guardian of this place, and looked at me calmly. 'This is why you are here,' he said, 'because of these three.' I regarded this being in astonishment. 'Yes,' he went on, 'study them. It is very worthwhile to do so. It is a good idea to intuit the secret of things in the way they appear.' I had accustomed myself to heeding the advice of beings of the elemental world, and so I began to consider the three trees. To do so I sat down at a place that was roughly equidistant from all three of them. Then I proceeded to draw what I could observe supersensibly of them, and this gave rise to pictures of three tree spirits. Since I was concerned with three entities, this took a while. Then I witnessed how the tree spirits began to emanate a sense of restlessness. It was as if they were calling to me something I had not been willing to hear before. As I engaged with their wishes, I heard them all speak together like a chorus: 'Look at the wood, at the wood, it is the foundation of our life. On that the other rests.' I asked them what they wanted to tell me about their wood. It was this question they had been waiting for, and immediately they began to speak. I could hardly keep up with transcribing it.

It is the wood, its substance, through which we spirits of the trees ascend and descend. We move within it as in a fluid. Our life is bound up with it. It is indeed our kingdom, our earth, just as you human beings have an earth, the human earth, which is your realm of experience. That's how we live in the wood. For us it is not solid but extremely permeable and alive. Within a tree it has very diverse regions, different zones, in each of which the spirits connected with it experience something completely different. Thus the wood of the twigs and branches is different from the wood of the trunk, and this in turn is different from the wood of which the roots are composed. But even the wood of the trunk has layers that must be distinguished from each other, each of which grants us tree spirits different experiences. It is not so hard for you as you may think to enter these different realms of experience. Try it. There are sounds and realms in the wood which you can easily experience. We see that it is easy for you to live your way in to these different spheres of the tree.

I was struck by what I had heard. As well as I could, I enlarged upon my drawing accordingly. But then I noticed that the tree spirits had not yet finished. They had only been waiting for a moment and then began to speak again.

But what connects the whole wood of a tree, and what really connects all trees, is something else. Behind all trees, and all qualities of wood, stands a being with whom the trees and all their spirits are deeply connected. This is the being of the living Christ. He lives in the wood because his blood, as he died, poured out over it. In consequence the wood has been subject to a special process. Since then it stands in a special relationship with the being of Christ. It enables him to exercise his process of transformation, which only began at the Resurrection. It is upon the trees that the being of Christ can rely unconditionally. The wood has already been redeemed whereas human beings are still in the process of transformation. Christ lives in the wood in a way that is different from how he lives in human souls. He has chosen the wood as his dwelling place. He is within it, whereas human souls are as yet still realizing him within them. Wood is a sanctified substance.

*

We can ask how the intrinsic nature of each tree species can be grasped. Once again, I would like to describe a personal experience here. In Soglio in Bergell, in the Swiss canton of Graubuenden, there is a terrace with a wonderful view over the valley across to the craggy, high mountains of its farther side. Taking the path down into the valley you pass sweet chestnuts that are husbanded with great care and expertise, and from which a harvest is gathered in the autumn. When walking there one day I encountered an especially striking example, an ancient tree that seemed to invite us to stay there with it for a while. Upon its trunk I found a place to sit, a throne, and sat down there. I clearly sensed that I was the guest of a mighty being—I found myself in a sphere of intense luminosity which continually rose from below and surrounded me. As I gazed into this light I looked into a realm of peace and equilibrium. It was as if I were relieved of all cares that troubled me, as if my soul were lulled and wrapped by an infinitely benevolent being, a great mother. I could not understand what was happening to me. It seemed to me—and I can find no other words for it—as if the gateway to the bright kingdom of the inner earth, to shambala, were opening. I felt how the sweet chestnut lends strength to surrender oneself to the ordering powers of one's own destiny, thus to the healing powers which the soul bears within it as its original certainty and wisdom—but which it does not wish to acknowledge. Perhaps we fear this truth, or perhaps we have lost this certainty that we are subject to a higher guidance...? Those who surrender to the sweet chestnut find that it closes our eyes to external things and opens our inner eyes to behold our own sacred being, which stands entirely safe within the flux of changing destiny! Yes, this place exists, where we stand safe and secure within our own destiny. The sweet chestnut gives us powers of soul that allow us to rest our attention upon our own sacred and wise being of soul. Here are words of the sweet chestnut's tree spirit:

> I guard the inner light of the earth for you human beings, to heal your wounded souls. They are wounded because they have accustomed themselves to earth existence, and suffer injury because, fine as they are, they are not always equipped to endure what they encounter, the pain, the privation, the fear, envy and malice. They do not know such things from their home of light and react in such alarmed ways therefore when they are compelled to see and experience how different things are on earth. And yet they know that the earth must become their home, and that they must arm themselves for this. I stand beside them when they do not know how to go on, thinking they can no longer bear the pain because they meet it unprepared. I let the healing, sacred light of the healed earth into their souls so that they may receive solace from her, the earth, their great mother, the goddess of destiny. The earth comforts them through me, so that they must no longer be deprived of the heavenly light of their soul home. This rises to them from the shrine of their deep soul life and through it they can become sound again.

*

This account can show that each species of tree embodies a spiritual gateway through which the human soul can step to gain access to very specific powers of soul. As member of a species, each tree—whether it is a blackthorn, a walnut, a yew—represents a doorway whose secret it wishes to divulge but which only does so if we understand how to coax this from it. This portal is most apparent to the super-sensible gaze in the realm of the roots, where the earth-ly-cosmic entrance to the secret being of the tree is found. The root is the gateway through which the supersensible gaze can penetrate to gain sight of the high powers that integrate each species of tree with the circle of all trees. In the example of the sweet chestnut what we can experience on passing through such a portal has been described. A corresponding description could be given for every other species—and then it would become apparent how deeply trees are connected with the earth on the one hand, and with the human being on the other. Their gifts are to do with the fact that they are beings who stand directly at the threshold of worlds. They raise their visible forms *out* of the earth. That they root in the earth means that the earth is their bodily mother. They are earth beings, not only of the physical earth but likewise of the spiritual earth. We are only gradually coming to know them as mediators, as mes-sengers of the spiritual earth. Their sublimely expressive forms are a picture through which they point us to their deeper being, the very ground of their nature.

Every gateway leads into a different spiritual land. The soul who knows how to pass through each portal can jour-ney through these different lands. It will bring back from such travels gifts that can become fruitful for its life on earth. From the sweet chestnut it receives the gift of confi-dence in destiny, from the ash courage for destiny, from the hornbeam trust, from the birch sensitivity, from the haw-thorn wisdom, from the blackthorn vigour and vitality, and from the walnut reverence for the past. These vague summaries—forgive me—are meant as no more than initial pointers to the gifts we can receive from other species of trees. They are offered only as stimulus for readers to pursue their own engagement with trees.

8
The spirits of the trees

Every tree spirit is a noble being. He regards the people who walk past beneath him or live in his vicinity. The tree spirit acquires his character from the species of tree he dwells in and the location where the tree stands. What happens around the tree affects and impinges on him.

The tree stands at a very specific place, and for the tree spirit this means that he is exposed to a very particular play of cosmic, earthly and historical forces. The soil in which a tree roots exerts a key influence upon its spirit, making both tree and spirit part of a dynamic that extends to the centre of the earth. Every tree is always also a gateway to powers that shine up out of the centre of the earth, in which the tree spirit naturally also shares. The tree spirits are beings through which a significant exchange always also occurs between the cosmos and the spirit form of the earth's interior.

The tasks of tree spirits are not confined to a single tree; they reach further to encompass human beings too, indeed to encompass humanity. The tree spirits fulfil their most sacred tasks in relation to the further evolution of the human race, attending both to trees and to human beings and their evolution. Below we will examine what is involved in this evolution.

*

Every tree spirit mediates currents of very distinct supersensible energies that ascend and descend between the earthly and the cosmic world. Every tree spirit does this in his own way. To discern his being, we have to explore the nature of these energy currents, which become manifest when we contemplate the nature of a particular tree species. At the same time the location of the tree, the region in which it grows, is also decisive, for it is this that confronts the tree spirit with the tangible earthly world in which he leads his life. Whether a tree stands in the middle of a village or in the forest or at a distinct place in a landscape affects the nature of the tree spirit and poses very particular tasks for him. Thus we can observe how the tree spirit of a willow standing beside a river is pervaded by the currents which, originating from the river's spring and mouth, are transmitted through the flowing water. The tree spirit of an oak standing lonely in a forest clearing, is very important for the elemental and also higher powers of the landscape where the tree is situated. At certain times it will be visited by elemental beings who gather beneath it. The tree spirit of an old larch in the mountains, far removed from human paths, serves ascending and descending human souls who leave the earth or arrive here for their next life. The beech tree beside a house which has witnessed a long and turbulent history, is guardian of what has occurred and still occurs there, both in and around the house. This tree spirit connects the different eras of the house, the various lives lived there. Thanks to its long life, in contrast to the elemental spirits of herbaceous plants, a tree spirit is able to exert a strong influence both in the landscape and amongst humankind. He attends to what happens amongst human beings in a town, a village or a house. The older a tree is, the greater the tasks which the spirit belonging to it can undertake. In this respect, the tree spirit of a young tree is an apprentice still.

It can be observed that the tree spirit of a young tree is subject mostly to the influence of the tree species. The tasks which a tree spirit takes on over the course of time suppress this influence. This can reach a stage where the latter becomes insignificant. In an old tree which has important tasks in the landscape, in the elemental world or the human world, the species itself plays only a subordinate role.

*

If we inwardly attune to the spirit of an old tree, we will notice that we have before us a very noble and surprisingly autonomous being. Usually this being will observe and examine us. In other words, he does not simply disclose his secrets but places conditions upon the one who seeks to communicate with him. This may mean initially that we meet with resistance and rejection. We will have to practise patience, persistence, and show real interest, to persuade a tree spirit to open himself to our human wishes and questions. Tree spirits can be really very strict and dismissive, something we repeatedly find to be the case with higher beings of the elemental world. We first have to make efforts to win the favour of these entities. True interest, deep empathy, and a sense of responsibility, are the bases for winning such favour. The tree spirit will examine human beings to see if they are worthy to gain knowledge of his secrets. It is very much in keeping with the noble nature of tree spirits that they undertake this scrutiny of us, basically testing each person's morality. The rigour of their gaze upon us shows them to be deeply pervaded by the world of spirit. They possess stores of wisdom which human beings must time and again seek to attain.

*

The entirety of trees and tree spirits form an encompassing circle around humanity. We can understand this circle in terms of moral powers that issue from the trees and their spirits. They speak very softly to us; really they whisper, but anyone who has once heard their voices will never again forget them. It is therefore a good exercise to develop our sense of morality in attunement with trees. They want the hearkening soul to become aware through them of its own moral forces. We can in fact approach different trees with the wish to perceive the moral power that speaks to the soul *through* them. The oak embodies a different morality from the rowan or the juniper. This may initially be apparent in the characteristic mood that every tree emanates. The oak absorbs the listening soul without reserve; the rowan points us to the sustaining power of truthfulness; the juniper shows the path the soul still needs to retrace to perceive its own, unquenchable light. A quite different prompting issues from each tree. We can sense that the trees wish to support us in discerning our own, living spirit germ. The circle of trees surrounds the human soul with a luminous garment of light that awakens the soul to its own morality.

*

As we approach the spirits of trees inwardly and attentively, we enter into a conversation for which our own inner hearing is not always mature enough. As yet we do not grasp the full import of what occurs between the spirit of a tree and ourselves, though we can sense that something essential is happening. We should not allow ourselves to feel discouraged by the fact that our conscious grasp encompasses only a fraction of what unfolds in this conversation.

Further periods of development will be needed before we can fully and consciously comprehend what occurs here. As yet we are still in the process of growing in to the reality of this conversation.

But we can clearly intimate that the beings of trees (and also of other plants, animals and landscapes) are waiting for us to continually refine our listening. The spirits of the trees wish to be heard. This is because a distinct spiritual substance forms through listening conversation. This substance is very delicate, very luminous, but anything other than weak. Where someone grows together inwardly with what surrounds them, perceiving what lives between them and the beings in their vicinity with wakeful interest and empathy, substance of this kind develops. It is a nourishing substance through which nature beings really can grow sound and well again. We can imagine that this substance arising through inward dialogue between the human being and nature falls as a healing light into the earth and is preserved there for the future.

No attentive listening is lost; no loving, sympathetic attention is in vain. The love that lives in interest for life's realities does not pass away but inscribes itself in the earth for the future, for times that still await both her and us. The tasks of the beings of the elemental world include the receiving and safekeeping of this substance. It is they who ensure that everything that happens on earth is incorporated into it. Their living entities connect what unfolds in time with the earth's spatial realm.

In this respect, the tree spirits have a key task. Their form penetrates space. They live within the earth, are bound up with wood, and raise themselves into the regions of the earth's air and light. It is understandable therefore that they have been our teachers since primordial times. In them lives something that spans and connects both space *and* time. They partake of both eternity *and* each moment. If we encounter them with enhanced perception, we can discover before us beings with something to tell us that goes beyond the moment. They connect now with the past. They form bonds between the ages, between evolutionary stages encompassing human beings and the earth. Their nobility is to do with the fact that they pass on through epochs, through cultures, not forgetting what has once occurred. In the same way they know what is still to come.

Trees are our siblings. They endow those who stay beside them and rest with them with gifts that strengthen, encourage and instruct. We leave a different person from the one who came there.

9

Plants, and trees, and the human soul

With death the soul overcomes the earth's substantiality as it lays the body aside. It enters spheres that it cannot perceive with bodily senses but which receive and absorb it now, after death. Beings of the higher worlds receive the soul and prepare it for the life to come. This means that the soul looks upon the earth for a while in a way unknown to it during earthly life: it beholds the earth through the sphere of willed actions accomplished in its previous life. A person now no longer perceives the earth with their senses but through the effects of their previous actions. In life after death, the soul orients itself by this means as it looks back upon the earth. During earthly life, we experience ourselves as autonomous beings in relation to the substantiality of the earth. In life after death the soul is granted sight of the earth through the deeds of its past life. The soul now beholds these deeds in the same way as, during earthly life, it beheld a natural occurrence or phenomenon—a storm, a waterfall or a crystal. They continue to belong to us but we behold them now from without.

Similarly the soul now likewise experiences the objects of its willed actions in a different way. These are no longer outward things but beings through which it beholds itself. Things which, for example, we once held in our hands, are now experienced as we previously experienced our own body in earthly life. They become organs of perception that enable us to look upon our own life. The flower we picked, the fire we lit, the animal we stroked, the wood we carved, the person we beheld are now experienced inwardly so that through them we regard ourselves. We behold the being we were in our past life through the objects to which our own willed actions were directed. Outward experience transforms into inward experience. Our purchase upon our past earthly reality is accomplished through an inward experience of the moments in which we connected ourselves, through an action, with a thing or entity of the earthly world. The world of things becomes a world of being in which the soul now lives as it previously lived in a human body. This leads to an intense experience of the earth and its beings, of minerals, plants, animals and human beings we met there.

The beings of nature which the soul perceived as something outward during its earthly life are experienced from within after death. If, during life, someone rode a horse, now they are the horse and experience themselves through it. If we loved someone, we now experience ourselves through what this other person experienced through us in earthly life. If we abused another person for our own ends, we now experience through this other person the force of manipulation we exerted on them, or the violence or injury we did to them. An experience of ourselves arises which connects us in illuminating fashion with ourselves and with the beings to whom our actions were directed. In this way we experience every being we encountered during earthly life. Through experiencing the consequences of our own deeds the earth becomes an inward experience for us: the soul connects with the earth now in a way that is possible only in exceptional cases during life on earth. The earth becomes inward within the soul. Thus for a person who has died the earth does not

disappear at all; far from it, she lives on in us in a different, inward way.

*

*After death, the soul encounters the spiritual strata of the living
being of the earth.* On its journey it passes through the realm
of living spiritual powers or beings, the etheric sheath of
the earth. This sheath permeates the world we know as
the sense- or physical world. Each thing belonging to the
earthly world is imbued and encompassed by the etheric
realm. Thus the human soul meets the spiritual beings
of the forces and substances that constitute the physical
world and thus the environment of living souls. In tangible
terms, this means that souls who have died live for a while
in the diverse elements—earth, water, air and warmth. In
this way they come to know the dynamic, earth-fertilizing
existence of the elemental beings. In other words, we can
truly say that the beings of the elemental world harbour or
shelter dead souls for a certain period.

*

*After death the soul is not only absorbed by the elements but also
by the trees.* It meets wood. Souls enter the tree through the
process of wood formation in the cambium, the life-bear-
ing layer of the tree. For souls it is a key stage of their
post-mortem path to experience the spiritual processes at
work in the development of wood. But at the same time
souls also connect with the resulting emergence of the
shape of a tree and the processes that allow the wood to die
and rot. From this perspective, wood is pervaded by the
interest and sympathy of human souls who are in the process of departing from the earth. They migrate through the

wood. And all processes of dying and rotting are encompassed in this interest.

We should not imagine that all wood is continually pervaded by such souls. It is rather that, on the journey after death, they waft through wood as well as other earth substances too. Wood is so attractive to souls who have died because they experience the secret of life and death through it. Through wood they learn how every death is the transition to another life. Trees show souls the threshold where they stand between life and death. Wood itself stands at this threshold, allowing ascending souls to deeply behold and comprehend the secret of life and death. They feel a longing for wood for in it they behold their own transformation.

*

What is true of wood is true too of all earthly substances, and naturally also of herbaceous plants, the flowering plants. In life after death, the soul gazes through plants upon the earthly world. During life it has regarded plants from without; now, as it were, it looks out of them upon earthly conditions. In a sense the soul is now more deeply and intimately bound up with the nature of plants than it was able to be during earthly life. In fact it experiences the plant's spirit being. It lives directly within the high being of particular plants. These experiences intensify if, in the soul's past life, it has had deep encounters with the plant world. Perhaps a specific plant has served to heal someone, or they have cultivated certain plants in their garden, or sold them at market and earned their living in this way. This shows that people are not as separate from the world of plants as they might think. Plants are beings that belong to our existence. We are deeply bound up with them but we can only understand the full scope of this connection if we behold the human soul as a spirit being.

The healing power of plants is founded in the deep relationship that exists between the human soul and the plants in the life after death. Plants are beings inherent in the human soul, and the human soul is likewise inherent in plant beings. We bear the plant beings and their affect in us because we are spirit beings like them. Threads spun between death and rebirth connect us with the nature of plants.

*

These thoughts lead us to picture the world of plants as a spiritual raiment which we receive from the world of spirit and in which we are mantled when we die, but also when we fall asleep. The world of spiritual plant beings has a relationship with the human being which we can describe as being wrapped in a spiritual garment as soon as our soul releases itself from the earthly context. This garment or cloak has a tangible supersensible form, for every plant occupies a very particular place in it. In meditation we can bring this plant mantle to mind by trying to picture the places which different plants occupy in it. Sage occupies the place where the cloak is fastened at the throat. Plantain lies lower, in the chest region; St John's-wort does not occupy a particular place but is woven through the whole cloak; the sunflower rests in the line that runs between the solar plexus and the forehead chakra; blackthorn and yarrow place themselves over the liver; hawthorn lies in the region of the heart, and lady's-mantle seeks out the place of the root chakra.

Through inward experience of this plant cloak we can recognize the relationship between plants and the human being. Plants belong to our being. A higher perspective shows that both are one. The nature of the human being is inconceivable without the plants, and vice versa. As we behold the plant world, we also behold a part of our own being, one that has become outward, certainly, but nevertheless intrinsically belongs to us. In sleep, and after death, this original unity is reinstated: we absorb the plant kingdom into ourselves again and, vice versa, the plant kingdom absorbs us once more.

10
Ways to know plants

Every plant affects and informs the soul in its own way. Something issues from plants that seizes hold of the observer, who senses they stand before a marvel that would change them if they could surrender themselves to it in the right way. We cannot relinquish the sense that plants want something from us! They do not only exist for themselves but every plant has a distinct and very particular relationship with the human being. They are close to us but it is not easy to understand this closeness. How can we attune to them and come to attend better through them?

Each plant manifests through its form, which discloses its unique nature and developmental laws. We observe this form when we study the shape of the blossom, the development of the leaves, when we smell the fragrance of its flower or taste its fruit, or feel the consistency of its stem, leaves or wood. Each plant belongs to a plant family, has a particular geographical spread, flowers at a particular time, forms its own unique pollen. All these observations together form what we can perceive of it with our senses. In doing so we call to mind the 'picture' of the plant. But the picture is not yet the being. In the picture I make of a plant I do, certainly, have expressions of its nature but have not grasped its essence. The picture of a plant relates to its intrinsic being like an outward garment. The being is something different, for as I approach it I enter a realm unavailable to sense perception. The being of a plant cannot be grasped through sense organs for it is supersensible in nature. Nevertheless the picture is a stage on the way to grasping its being.

Now we can assume that people continually encounter spirit beings but are unaware of this. Our feeling life consists of these encounters but they do not reach our conscious mind. We always also meet a plant as a feeling human being, but the consequences this has for us usually remain unconscious. But the soul is touched by a flowering, fragrant lavender bush, or by an oak tree beneath which we rest. They make an impression on the soul. Every encounter with a plant has its very particular reverberations. It is an interesting exercise to try to become aware of such influences. We are continually exposed to impressions, and we can try to attend to their further resonance in us. A storm, rain, sudden cold and darkness, lightning and thunder do not pass us by without a trace. Meetings with other people, too, sometimes go on reverberating in the soul for days afterwards, as do scenes from films, or photographs, or also tales we hear or stories we read. Occurrences, even supposedly unimportant ones, always leave an echo in us. And this is true too of course for plants.

*

Plants speak in gestures. As we observe and inwardly re-experience the gestures displayed by a plant or a tree, we receive a deep impression of its spirit being. The plant reveals itself to our sense perception through the manifold gestures of its growth forms. It is all gesture: its flowers, its leaves, the shapes it has assumed as it grows. It is just a matter of allowing these to resonate vividly in the soul. There is a 'gestural sense' through which every impression goes on echoing in us. For studying the being of a plant it is important to discover this echo and practise engaging with it. The beings of plants reveal themselves to the human soul through this reverberating echo. By discovering the soul's ability to resonate in this way, and refining it, we will come to know the language of plants and of trees.

Through their picture, their gestures, plants give us signs of their hidden being. This is unavailable to our outer senses but speaks to our inner ones. Only *within* ourselves do we find the 'listener' to whom the outer world can speak.

*

We can speak of the soul of a plant, which underlies its outward and perceptible form. And we can enter into dialogue with it, as *from soul to soul!* We can ask it things, as we would ask a question of another person or ourselves, thus holding an inner conversation. This requires a certain courage, as well as trust and a spirit of enquiry, certainly. But it is well worth conversing directly with a plant. It will reply! Just often not in the way we may be expecting. But we possess many undiscovered capacities, only a small portion of which we are as yet aware of. The plants, these seemingly silent companions of our lives, wish to instruct us, wish to teach us about the capacities we have not yet discovered.

To approach the spirit being of a plant requires inner work, for we must listen with our inner senses. Within us lies a realm that resonates with the plant being. This work is one I myself must undertake, and requires patience and practice, for it is a path to my own unique experiences. This does not mean that science does not need it, but we are on a dangerous path if we think that gaining knowledge is an exclusively external matter that can be delegated to experts. Cognition is an archetypally human activity, hence one that each person must conduct for themselves.

It is good to give sufficient time to our engagement with a particular plant, to repeatedly observe it, study its outward form, to draw it, smell its scent and taste it—thus to keep turning to it. Then we will notice that our relationship to the plant changes: it becomes familiar; over time we become acquainted, and will keep discovering new things. If it is a medicinal plant it is also good to make oneself a remedy from it. You can make oils, Bach flower remedies, tinctures, ointments—and thus come to know many aspects of the plant. A time will come when it speaks to you! You will feel its proximity to you because you know it well. With time you will know the 'feel' of various plants. You feel the strength in arnica, the deep love in St John's-wort or the strictness of yarrow—the soul of the plant.

*

In this process we can become accustomed to trusting our intuitions. The capacity for intuition is a deeply human quality. All of us possess it, varying only in degree and scope. Intuitions usually arise in activities or concerns in which we are present with heart and soul. But intuitive perception is also elicited when we open ourselves to something without preconception.

*

Our own hands are also organs of perception; they can perceive as if they had eyes. They can develop a sensitivity capable of experiencing the essential nature of things and substances. We can develop this sensitivity, for example, by placing a fresh calendula blossom in the palm for a while,

and observing any bodily and soul reactions. It is necessary to ensure that we are not going to be disturbed while
we do so, and that we are calm and tranquil. Pressing daily
concerns impair our observations or make them impossible since the soul then lacks the stillness to focus on its
observations. If we observe carefully we will notice that
our body responds to the contact of the flower in its palm.
We can refine and enhance these observations and extend
them to other flowers and parts of plants. Take care when
observing poisonous plants since they can trigger very
unpleasant reactions. In general the amount of a plant
sample should not be excessive, even for non-poisonous
plants, and the observations should be ended if you start
feeling unwell.

*

*We will find that the body responds to every plant in a unique
way.* Calendula acts upon body and soul in one way,
milk-thistle, St John's-wort and lady's mantle in another.
When you start to practise this work of perception, the
bodily reactions may only be mild and subtle. As your sensitivity increases the mode of action of different plants will
become ever more clearly perceptible and unmistakeable.
With time it can become sufficient to touch a plant only
momentarily, or to look at it for a short while only, before
reactions at the level of body and soul become apparent.

These observations show that plants exert an influence
on the state of our consciousness. Some have a soporific
effect, since they enhance the connection of our consciousness with the bodily level, whereas others release the mind
from the body so that it gains an impulse to attend more
alertly to surrounding occurrences. There are plants that

can truly be said to strengthen our powers of consciousness and to open us to higher dimensions of our own being.

If we become acquainted with plants in this intimate way, we will be surprised to find how each can instruct us. Every plant points the human soul to a very particular aspect of its nature. To experience this connection between the soul of a plant and the human soul is one of the deepest experiences available to us. And then we know that plants have a deep affinity with us.

11
The nature of certain plants and trees

The flowering plants are our siblings, beings who belong to us because they can redress what we sunder from harmony, what we make disharmonious and are unable to heal ourselves. The harm we cause can be healed by plants. They possess powers which we cannot ourselves easily incorporate, powers that have left us. We would not need the plants if plant existence were within us instead of outside us. We are human beings because we are no longer plants, because we have been robbed of our plant nature. And we are therefore all the more dependent on the beings whose distinguishing characteristic is to have remained plants. When we incline to plants we are always inclining to ourselves, to a part of our own being that has been taken from us so that we could evolve as humankind. We have had to overcome our plant nature to develop consciousness, in the process losing what we receive from plants as the gift of healing forces. Through plants we find our way back to ourselves because through them we participate in what we have been deprived of in order to become earthly human beings. They reveal our whole nature to us, the original unity of our being, our cosmic nature. In turning to them we can discover that they speak to us of our great, original nature. It is as if they wished to say this to us:

> O man, do not forget what you had to relinquish to become a human being on earth. We are yours; you regard us as a stranger and yet are deeply familiar to

us. We belong to you, wish to accomplish and fulfil with you the work of earth that is our common mission. Accept us as your soul sisters, who seek to heal you of the error that what you behold in yourselves is everything you are. We are the More which belongs to you; we show you your being whose boundaries extend far beyond what you believe yourselves only to be.

*

Every plant that we observe carefully can be experienced as a spiritual portal we can approach and through which we can pass. We can feel that the plant offers us a threshold that does not repulse us but invites us to make an inward gesture to cross it. For the soul, the plant is anything other than an insuperable barrier. After vividly picturing the plant before our inner eye, we 'enter' into it with full awareness, reaching the 'other side' of the plant, thus the place from where issue the spiritual forces that produce and create it. We enter the 'soul land' from which the plant originates spiritually, thus the spiritual reality represented by the plant within the earthly sphere. In other words, we receive an impression of the soul aspects that are safeguarded by a particular plant. Naturally, practice is needed to cross this threshold; it will not succeed at the first attempt. But if you take time and proceed with care and respect, you may be able to gain initially faint yet perceptible impressions which without doubt point to the soul nature of each plant. In this way one receives very different impressions from different plants. We pass through the picture of the plant's physical form, as through a living spiritual picture, and surrender ourselves consciously to the being of the plant. We must be completely open to whatever occurs on the other side of the portal. Usually inner pictures will surface, and we have to try to discern them without adding to them anything of our own. Below I will describe the ways in which certain plants have a soul affinity with human beings.

*

The dog-rose opens the way to our own, sacred soul-child. This is the aspect of our soul that is always bright and sure, that can never be seized by darkness and always remains connected with the highest hierarchies of the world of spirit. The rose helps when we have a feeling that we are losing touch with ourselves, losing a connection with the higher being we are.

*

The larch is a tree which makes available to us a power that reaches deep into our living organism. This supports the human personality, our I, in being present within our own body. An awakening power comes to effect that mediates between a person's high spirit impulses and their organism, making it easier to realize the lofty and pure motives and impulses we bear within us. The power of the larch helps our individuality to remain true to itself despite obstacles that seek to prevent us truly acting out of ourselves. It helps us to remain steadfast, and above all to stand up for what we ourselves believe and intend. Larch is indicated when we feel inhibited from acting autonomously because outer obstacles appear too powerful.

*

Inula or yellowhead is a plant that helps a person learn to live with the dark or evil aspects of their personality. To accept the whole of ourselves is work we continually face. In its entirety my being encompasses dark aspects. My doubts, fears, negative feelings such as jealousy, rage, aggression, malice, are integral to my being, and I have to consider how to deal with them. Inula is a very strong plant which mediates the strength to face up to our dark aspects and to remain steadfast in the face of them. To stand firm before the powers of evil in our own soul does, however, require a great capacity of perseverance, a great deal of courage since beholding this darkness in ourselves can rob us of self-confidence and self-trust. Inula mediates the courage to keep on trusting even when this trust in ourselves seems under great threat. It is indicated in situations in which we despair because we feel ourselves succumbing to the powers within us that would rob us of the right to go on living.

*

St John's-wort is a plant with deep effects. It connects the soul with the level of the blood. It calls upon the soul to connect with powers through which an individual can be reconciled with themselves. This reconciliation encompasses all aspects of the individuality, including those that originate in former lives and therefore play into us in unconscious and hidden ways. These are very unconscious aspects of the soul, active in the blood which, if not in some way accepted and affirmed by the soul, can start to play havoc. This can come to expression, for instance, in depression. St John's-wort supports us in finding the strength unreservedly to affirm ourselves and our destiny.

*

The mullein or Aaron's Rod imparts to the human soul a strength that enables it to realize its higher nature and the aspect of futurity connected with it. Our higher being always also works toward us out of the future. The mullein enhances our attentiveness to the luminous sheath that wraps every soul in a starry mantle. This increases our trust and confidence in taking further steps out of ourselves, out of our own impulses and intrinsic being. The spiritual protection in which we stand becomes discernible experience, and encloses the soul in a peaceful light so that we are relieved of our mean-spirited and narrow qualities. In their place stirs the certainty that we will cope with every situation that destiny brings us. We feel that we have been given all that we need to join our own star with the earth and her destiny. The power of mullein mediates the confidence that earth is our birthright, that we belong here, and therefore can continually engage further with the earth.

*

The nature of milk-thistle works deeply into the human organism. When we connect with it meditatively, we feel ourselves being transformed from within. The power of milk-thistle works down into the level of single cells. For the soul the effect of this is to feel absorbed, accepted, by corporeal nature—it sleeps into the body, as it were. But this feeling, surprisingly, does not lead to a dullness or torpidity spreading in the soul. On the contrary, the soul awakens, awakens to itself. The soul, our individuality in fact, becomes aware of itself as a being who possesses the duty and strength to be self-determining. What rises in the soul through contact with the being of the milk-thistle is a mighty power that enables an individual to make their own resolves and decisions. Ultimately this plant accompanies us in the development through which we become ever truer to ourselves. The paths leading to this congruity and self-realization are never easy, simple or comfortable: they are complex, steep and arduous, but despite possible appearances, not a detour or diversion. The milk-thistle imparts the sustained effort and endurance we need on our path through life.

*

White hellebore is a poisonous mountain plant. For the soul it embodies a being who protects us at times of great danger. When we live our way in to its nature, we become aware of a protective gesture upon which we can call even in acute cases of threat and fear. When we have the feeling that the ground has been taken from under our feet, white hellebore always still offers assurance and safety. If we know that we tend to such states, we can meditate upon the nature of this plant. Having, as it were, inwardly 'filled ourselves to the brim' with this plant, we will be well prepared when we need it. But for this we must devote ourselves to it intensively over a certain period. It can also happen that a certain disgust or aversion toward this plant arises as we meditate on it. If so, then we know that we have 'arrived' fully with the plant, right down to the bodily level, and have really surrendered to it.

*

Hawthorn is a tree of contemplation. The soul grows tranquil, still, and attuned to its inwardness. A cave seems to form that shuts off everything that would distract or disturb the soul in its inward preoccupation. The soul is led to itself.

Hawthorn enhances the soul's concentration upon what lives within it spiritually, upon the core of its being that does not derive from the earth but is, rather, a child of the heavens. Hawthorn stimulates the soul's inner vision; the soul is led to behold the higher beings who create the life of the earth. It can therefore be considered a tree of initiation into life's higher mysteries.

*

Masterwort or astrantia is a great help in states of bodily weakness. This plant supplies the body with enlivening powers, prompting it not to succumb to weakness but to summon its forces and grow stronger. It lends the aura a protective, strong and bright luminosity that strengthens us and invokes our defences. Masterwort is indicated in situations in which we are exposed to attacks and opposition which we do not feel strong enough to deal with. Even a premonition of this kind of thing can sap our strength, and masterwort can help here too. Masterwort mobilizes our forces of resistance, blunting the power of situations to overwhelm us.

*

Hornbeam is a special tree which leads the human soul into the region of its pre-birth experience. It allows the soul to descend into the peaceful world in which it lived prior to all contact with conditions of earthly life. There it was guarded by spirit beings, growing toward life on earth until all was ready for it to be born. The hornbeam also wakens great trust in the earth; the soul feels how it is sustained and also guided through earth existence. Even if much that comes toward it is undependable, uncertain and unclear, the earth abides, sustaining our life, endowing us with life's great rhythms. The hornbeam teaches us that the earth is a motherly being, essential for human evolution. It is the tree of trust in life and in our own destiny.

*

The being of Christ belongs to the deepest mysteries hidden in the forms of the sense world. Supersensible vision shows that the being of Christ is to be found in the various aspects of the plants, primarily of course in their flowers. By approaching the being of the diverse flowers with devotion, we can have experiences that reveal different aspects of the being of Christ. Through flowering plants, in fact, we can gain access to the Christ being if we only hearken to what each flower speaks to the soul, touching it and seeking to transform it. Every flower is transformative, mediating a very particular message to the human soul. The soul can surrender to the life of spirit that works through every blossom. This conscious devotion can extend over a longer period, over several weeks. I would like to give three examples to show what I mean by this.

*

Chicory reveals a very important aspect of the Christ being, that is, a feminine aspect. In surrendering to the chicory flower I become aware of the feminine nature living in Christ. This is a feminine quality that entirely safeguards another's freedom yet offers everything which they need for their development—a selfless feminine nature, announcing itself in this wonderful blossom. For itself it desires only to remain free. That is, it rejects everything from which dependencies might arise. Support and nurturing of another human being should never give rise to new, constricting ties. On the contrary, it should help create free spaces, opportunities through which the other becomes able to renew their life.

*

The next flower we will consider in this context is arnica. In this, too, a key aspect of the Christ being lives. Arnica grows in the high mountains and is extremely resilient. Its flower is frequently unkempt and tousled. It is a plant that embodies the strength that awakens through resistance, which in a sense is the epitome of resistance. Arnica appeals to the soul forces through which resistance is transformed. Things that disturb, hinder, resist and counteract natural order should not be dismissed or rejected; it is much more useful to encompass and integrate them, although without giving their contrariness full rein. The strength of arnica consists in absorbing and thus transforming what seems to evade integration. Its palpable wildness shows that it has a direct access to chaos and the power of destruction, but does not allow itself to be mastered by this.

*

The third flower to be considered here is Echinacea or purple coneflower. As we look at it we can discover that it is connected with the secret implicit in every human soul, every human life, indeed every human individuality. In this plant resounds the miracle of our inner being. It mediates powers of deep transformation to the human soul. It points the way to divine powers available to every person. Each of us is connected with the being of Christ simply by virtue of being human. The path to Christ is not long and arduous, nor dependent on particular conditions. He is here and available to every person of goodwill. The Echinacea flower mediates a deep strength, a primordial trust that includes our own trust in ourselves. The soul who feels weak, burned out, empty and sad can find comfort with it. This flower is a great healer of the soul who seeks inner orientation.

12
Animal and human being

In former times human beings knew of the high spiritual mission of animals. Traditional legends and fairy tales have kept this knowledge alive down to our own times. Animals were revered because people knew that they embody particular configurations and contexts relating to the human being and our connection with the forces at work in the cosmos. They knew that animals always also show something that belongs to us. In every animal lives something that points beyond human life. They embody in tangible form the fact that we are part of a greater existence encompassing the cosmos and the earth. Animals were perceived in olden times as beings that mediate between worlds. They walk beside us, accompanying our path, and they can do so because they have not lapsed to the degree that we have from the great web of existence. They are messengers that connect us with the realm that we have departed from.

Today, too, an intimate perception of the nature of animals can remind us that our being has a deep connection with the powers and beings of the cosmos. They embody forces in which we participate, certainly, but do so in a largely unconscious way. In our era human consciousness is so emancipated that it does not so easily discern its participation in the powers of the cosmos any more. We can lead our lives without having to pay heed to the fact that we are children, offspring, of the cosmos. Instead we experience ourselves as autonomous and self-determining individuals. But the danger is that we lose our connection with the spiritual cosmos. Growing self-possession is an unavoidable part of our development but we should not omit steps on this path that help us to remember our spiritual origins. Animals cannot lose their connection with the cosmos, but this means at the same time that they cannot evolve into autonomous creatures. They have never left behind them what we had to leave behind us in order to become free beings. The experience of being separate from the cosmos is one unknown to them.

*

Through every animal the cosmos speaks in a particular way. They are messengers for those who do not shy away from observing them with eyes of soul. They convey to us what we had to leave behind us on our evolutionary path and will regain once more in freedom. Those who hearken to animals can discover that they are waiting for the human being to develop this freedom and act out of it, for this is something unavailable to them. They want us to do this for them. The freedom human beings acquire is also acquired for them. Eventually human beings will reincorporate the wisdom that informs the life and behaviour of animals. But to do so we must first pass through the probations that face us. Only then will animals share with us their perfection, the immediacy of their connection with the cosmos.

The inclination to place animals below us in a hierarchy of being is the expression of a process of evolution through which humankind severs its umbilical cord with the world of spirit. By raising ourselves above animals we set in stone something that is only a transitional reality. The animals have tasks which, like the tasks of humankind, surpass

what they momentarily reveal to us, whose full scope will
only be fulfilled in future.

Today contempt for the world of animals has reached its
nadir. Human beings grant themselves the right to regard
animals as nothing but 'production factors', as mere objects
in fact. This stance can only come about through our fail-
ure to recognize the spiritual forms of the animals.

*

The silver cauldron of Gundestrup found in Denmark in 1891 is
an eloquent example of the lofty significance which human
beings once accorded the animal kingdom. In our context,
consideration of this ritual object is so revealing because
it shows us that people once regarded animals as helper
beings, from whom they gained important impulses for
their own spiritual evolution. The cauldron depicts animals as creatures standing *above* the human level, without whom we could not attain our human nature. Our
relationship to animals is here seen as one in which the
latter bear the human being between them, seen from a
higher perspective. They make available to us forces that
are indispensable for us if we are to attain our human dig-
nity. This perspective is depicted on the cauldron in the
form of an antlered human being amidst a great host of
diverse animals. The eyes of the antler-bearer are closed,
his mouth is open and, with his legs crossed, he seems to
be listening rapt, with a special attentiveness. His left hand
holds a snake whose mouth almost touches his cheek, and
in his right hand he holds a torc, an open ring, whose open,
spherical ends lie over his larynx. The antlers springing
from his head resemble the antlers of the deer who stands
next to him and regards him. A series of other animals are

The silver cauldron of Gundestrup (section)

visible too: horn-bearing animals, beasts of prey, a dog and a fish with a rider.

No doubt it is difficult for us modern human beings to understand the images on the Gundestrup cauldron, since it is hard for us to transpose ourselves back into the state of consciousness of people of those times. Any interpretations should therefore be very cautious. Only sympathetic, thorough and sustained pondering can help disclose its meaning. We can get a sense that the human antler-bearer is listening to the animal beings surrounding him. We can feel how close his relationship with them is: their nature is an open book to him. Perhaps we can say that they gain a voice through him—we can imagine hearing them speak through his open mouth. At all events, this image is a striking example of the intimate relationship between the human being and the world of animals. It can show us how externalized our connection with them has become, and what experiential possibilities we have thereby lost. This antler-bearer can be envied for his inward listening, for the attentiveness which he elicits from the animal world.

*

The initiates of indigenous peoples felt the greatest reverence for animals. Mircea Eliade speaks of this in his book *Shamanism: Archaic Techniques of Ecstasy.*[4] Animals helped the shamans to perfect their esoteric knowledge. Through particular techniques which they had to practise for many years, shamans placed themselves into a state of consciousness that unlocked the language of the animals for them. Eliade writes:

> All over the world learning the language of animals, especially birds, is equivalent to knowing the secrets of nature and hence to being able to prophesy. Bird language is usually learned by eating snake or some other reputedly magical animal. These animals can reveal the secrets of the future because they are thought to be receptacles for the souls of the dead or epiphanies of the gods. Learning their language, imitating their voice, is equivalent to the ability to communicate with the heavens. [...] Birds are psychopomps. Becoming a bird oneself or being accompanied by a bird indicates the capacity, while still alive, to undertake the ecstatic journey to the sky and the beyond. Imitating animal voices, using this secret language during the seance, is yet another sign that the shaman can move freely through the three cosmic zones: underworld, earth, sky.

Those who stand close to nature through instinctive, empathic experience, will bring only the greatest respect toward animals, and in no way will they feel themselves entitled to look down on them. We can acknowledge them to be beings in every way equal to the human, on the one hand serving us through their very existence but at the same time owed our obligation and service. If we feel a lively and inward connection with the natural world, we know that we can only eventually become perfect through animals. We know that the animals are a world full of wisdom that contains mysteries we can only receive if we stand humble before their lawfulness.

In this context is it very interesting to consider the relationship of indigenous peoples to the animals they hunt. In their book about the shamans of northern Eurasia, Hans Findeisen and Heino Gehrts offer striking accounts:

> For that early humanity for whom hunting is culturally characteristic, our compulsion to eat, and the attendant need to kill other living creatures in order to consume their bodies, was seen as the great culpability of humankind! And it is in this general culpability of creaturely life, which appears as decidedly parasitic compared to the, in this respect, pure and guiltless plant world, that we can seek the ultimate source of the sense of human suffering and guilt cultivated by the great religions, especially Buddhism and Christianity. In this human culpability arising from the need to kill we may discover the source of the general hope of redemption that has come to expression in so many religions. Certainly, hunting is primordially associated with such guilt. The need to kill, in all its cruel necessity and ugliness, was such a common experience

of ancient hunters that it inevitably confronted them with terrible problems of conscience [...]. They know that they must kill animals to survive but the guilt they incur by doing so is such a burden for them that it must be redeemed again in some way. The example of the bear in northern legends can illustrate ancient traditions surrounding hunting that have survived into our own times. The bear is [...] not seen to be like other animals. Its fur only [...] represents a kind of disguise concealing a human form endowed with divine strength and wisdom. Everywhere in northern Eurasia, legends speak of the very distinctive qualities of the bear: his ability not only to hear what is being said about him from a great distance, but even to read the thoughts that people have of him. Thus the bear lies in wait for someone who thinks ill of him, and perhaps seeks to kill him, and brings misfortune to them, or even death.[5]

In these traditions, killing a bear requires adherence to particular rituals. After a successful hunt, the hunters undergo a purification rite, in winter covering themselves in snow, and in summer with earth, or spraying one another with water:

> In these rites, the greatest respect is shown to the body of the bear for his shade requires this. One must not mock him or make any disrespectful movement in his presence since the bear sees and hears everything, and will mercilessly punish those who display such conduct. But he holds human beings less strictly to account for his bodily 'death', since the northern Eurasian outlook is possibly more spiritual than almost any other on the earth. Only the 'soul' is truly essential

in all living creatures, and its separation from the body is not troublesome for it.

Strict rules apply to actions following the killing of the bear. His fur is regarded as the embodiment of his soul, and thus the greatest reverence is shown it. The skin is carried into the village, accompanied by songs, and is treated as a noble guest, and given a place of honour in the hunter's house. A festival is held with the aim of consoling and reconciling the soul of the dead bear. Only then is the owner of the fur allowed to sell it.

*

In Finnish mythology, as recorded in the Kalevala, *most of Rune 46 is devoted to the killing and eating of the bear.*[6] It is noteworthy that the moment when the bear is killed is scarcely apparent. The passage runs:

> Then the aged Vänämöinen
> Struck the bear where he was lying,
> Overturned his bed of satin,
> Overthrew his lair so golden.

The death of a bear could hardly be described more quietly. Then Vänämöinen, the bear-killer, tries to persuade his victim to accompany him, treating him as if he were still alive:

> Gazed he on the golden booty,
> And he spoke the words which follow:
> O my Otso, O my darling,
> Fair one with the paws of honey,
> Be not filled with causeless anger,
> I myself have not o'erthrown thee,

Thou thyself hast left the forest,
Wandered from thy pine-tree covert,
Thou hast torn away thy clothing,
Ripped thy grey cloak in the thicket.
Slippery is this autumn weather,
Cloudy are the days and misty.
Golden cuckoo of the forest,
Shaggy-haired and lovely creature,
Do thou quit thy chilly dwelling,
Do thou quit thy native desert
And thy home of birchen branches,
Wattled wigwam where thou dwellest.
Go to wander in the open,
O thou beauty of the forest,
On thy light shoes wandering onward,
Marching in thy blue-hued stockings,
Leaving now this narrow dwelling,
Depart and join the mighty heroes,
Leave and join the race of men!
There are none will treat thee badly
And no wretched life awaits thee.
For thy food they'll give thee honey
And for drink of mead the freshest
For the guest who new arrives now
From his long-awaited journey.

Here too it becomes apparent how the death of the animal
is veiled to avoid angering the lofty soul of the bear.

13
Encounters with animals

Destiny can lead people to deep encounters with animals. In her book *Listening to Whales, What the Orcas Have Taught us,*[7] Alexandra Morton describes one such encounter. She was travelling with her husband in a boat equipped with underwater microphones to track a group of killer whales that she had been observing for decades. Suddenly a thick fog enveloped them unexpectedly. She writes:

> Jeff and I could have been in a glass of milk. The water, smooth as honey, had no wave pattern to read. The sun had disappeared entirely. And Jeff and I had no compass. [...] Panic crept up my body. I knew exactly where we were: that was the problem. We were in the wide Queen Charlotte Strait, north of Hanson Island. Which meant that if we struck north, south, or east, we'd eventually find coastline. If we guessed wrong and headed west, I thought we wouldn't sight land until Japan.
>
> Over the hydrophone I picked up the throb: of a giant cruise ship. The suddenness of the sound meant that the ship had rounded the corner out of Blackney Passage, a major shipping lane, and was headed our way. We knew it came from the south. But where was south? The nondirectional hydrophone couldn't tell us. Our ears might eventually pick up the sound of the ship, but the fog was so thick, we might not hear it until just before its props churned us under.
>
> [...] Then, out of nowhere, a smooth black fin appeared. And another. Here was the big male Top

Notch, the familiar mother Saddle, the shy matriarch Eve, their fins spread like a hand of cards beside our boat. Stripe, Corky's mother, peeked at me just above the water's surface. Confidence washed the fear clean out of me. The presence of the whales wrapped me like a warm embrace. Instinctively I knew what to do. We would stay with the whales. Looking back, I don't understand the source of this confidence, as the whales had been heading out to sea all day.

[...] For the next twenty minutes, Jeff and I followed the pod. They stayed tightly clumped around the boat, swimming shallow so we could see them underwater. Sharky and Saddle swam so close that I shifted the engine into neutral several times so the propeller wouldn't cut them. The entire family surfaced beside us in a fan of dorsal fins.

In time a tiny islet revealed itself as a faint pattern in the fog. I couldn't be sure it was real; once you lose your focus in heavy fog, your eyes can play tricks on you. As its outline took on substance, though, the whales disappeared. Jeff and I sped full-throttle toward the ancient cedars and rocky coastline. Just before we reached land, the fog bank cleared and we burst into a glorious rosy sunset. I recognized the island. The whales had taken us south toward Blackney Pass—they had taken us back home. I idled the boat at the edge of the fog bank and waited. I knew they were only a couple of hundred feet behind me. But they had vanished.

[...] Had Jeff and I just been rescued? Was that possible? I'd heard stories of dolphins pushing drowning people to shore—tales going back to the time of Aristotle—but until that day I had discounted them as wishful myths. Science wasn't the neat and tidy experience I had expected. There was more here than mere numbers could represent. I can't say that whales are telepathic—I can barely say the word—but I'm unwilling to ignore what I've seen with my own eyes. Did they somehow sense my terror? I have no explanation for that day's events. I have only gratitude and a deep sense of mystery that continues to grow to this day.

*

Animals can also intervene in human destiny. Here's one example.

Aldo Leopold... reports how, as a young park ranger in the USA's south-western mountains, he had ridden up a mountain and looked down from the top on a falling stream. In the water he saw three wolves, a female with two grown cubs. Without thinking, they pulled their guns from the holsters and shot at the creatures. Back then, explains Leopold, it was natural to kill wolves, which were regarded simply as wild vermin. They hit the female, the two young ones escaped, and they galloped down on their horses just in time to see the animal die. Leopold saw the green fire in the eyes of the female wolf going out. He had believed it was fine to kill wolves since this would mean an increase in the numbers of red deer in the region, and benefit hunting. But at that moment he felt that the mountain itself did not approve this idea. It saw things differently from Leopold. He felt this disapproval of the mountain, as representative of the whole living context there, suddenly weighing upon him. From that moment on, as he writes, he knew that he had to learn to think like a mountain.[8]

*

The earth is inconceivable without animals. They enliven and pervade it, and give earthly reality a very particular and indispensable character. They flit and whirr through the air, burrow through the soil, swim through the waters of the oceans and rivers, migrate for long distances through the air and over the land, unite with blossoms, rest for months in the earth, and show an affinity with light and warmth. The diversity of their life forms and bodily shapes is almost infinite. What becomes visible through them will repeatedly astonish those who observe them in detail.

When we encounter an animal and observe it, we can feel ourselves to be face-to-face with a mysterious being. It moves, acts, displays activity in ways that we do not immediately understand. Where do its guiding impulses originate? What causes an ant to go where it does? What makes the blackbird sing in the early morning? Why does a grazing horse suddenly raise its head and gallop off, seemingly without reason? What makes a flock of wild geese migrate southwards? Why do bees fly to particular flowers? Creatures display behaviours that can be described but not so easily understood. An animal stands within reality in a way that seems unreachable to us. It is always a part of the whole earth. It does not raise itself above the laws of Creation but remains inherent in the earth's existence.

*

But what is the living experience of a horse, a swallow, a frog? How can we picture or imagine the soul life of animals? How do they themselves experience reality? It quickly becomes apparent that these questions can only be answered if we invoke the soul capacity of empathy, a power or gift that we possess. It is possible for us to learn to surrender ourselves to what lives around us, in which we participate through our senses, and to gain experiences in this way that can help us to discern essential qualities. We possess the active gift of empathy with other living beings, including animals. We need only start to develop this and apply it. Over time this ability will become for us an important source of first-hand experiences and thus of insights. We will come to see that the inner world of another living creature is not closed to us but can become as familiar to us as our own. Naturally this gift of empathy is dependent on certain conditions that will help us gain authentic experiences. We will have to school ourselves to reach a certain degree of selflessness and independence so as to refine our own soul into a faithful tool of perception.

Our encounters with animals can elicit in us the desire to develop our inner, soul senses. Without doing so, we will fail to understand the animals. Then they will remain alien to us, and we may tend to dismiss the idea that each possesses its own inner life.

With the soul capacity of empathy a person can intuit the nature of an animal, and feel something of its experience. We can 'become' an animal for a while, by allowing it to guide us in our sense of it. We can yield to its being, entrust ourselves to it. In doing this, we enter a realm of experience that we do not otherwise know. We relinquish the standpoint we usually have as a person. Only then do we discover that every animal has a cosmic dimension that distinguishes it from the human being. With every animal to which we surrender we are feeling our way into a state of consciousness that is pervaded by lofty wisdom. With every animal we enter a particular cosmic sphere. As this happens we will feel blessed, invigorated, and even in a sense perceived and recognized. This can awaken the sense that a bond is being renewed that always existed, but which we only now perceive as a deep truth: the bond uniting animal nature and humanity from primordial beginnings. By this means worlds open that may previously have been foreign to us but which are in fact worlds of peace, of union, of joyfulness.

*

It seems as if we ourselves were likewise animals once upon a time, and that we are not separated from them in the way we have hitherto assumed. It becomes apparent that, like the plants, animals too are our soul siblings. But they stand one level closer to us than the plants: through them shines something that touches us profoundly because it relates to our inmost secret—our I, our individuality.

14
Christ and the animals

The kingdoms of nature, the world of animals, of plants and of minerals, are mysterious books. They are written in a spiritual script that is inaccessible to object consciousness. They only disclose themselves when we perceive and read their sensory forms and gestures as signs that relate to their meaning as letters do to the meaning of a word. A word can never be understood from the letters that form it but only through the meaning to which they point. Every such meaning is supersensible in nature, as is the meaning which the books of life embody.

In every animal wise powers reveal themselves through its mode of life, its way of being, and are connected with the earth, the human being and the cosmos. An animal never stands alone; it has no knowledge whatsoever of our human isolation. A cow does not think as a human being does; rather the earth thinks in her. Her whole existence is the expression of lofty powers of wisdom. A bird does not sing only for itself: through it resounds a song that pervades it and whose origin does not lie within the creature itself, but elsewhere. And the effect and reverberation of its song is not only meaningful for the bird but also for the whole life of the region where it resounds. The song of a bird streams through it: it is the instrument through which this song reveals itself and takes effect.

We cannot regard an animal in the same way as we regard a human being, for it does not lapse from the cosmos; it remains a part of the spiritual totality of the earth. An animal has no knowledge of the source of distinctive human capacities, which is our self-awareness. The consciousness of the animal is one with the powers which stream through earth into earthly life from the cosmos. The animal is intimately connected with the whole cosmos and has no knowledge of the form of consciousness of the human I.

*

The nature and organism of the cow can only be understood if we behold the powers with which she is connected. For supersensible observation there is no doubt that the cow's organization is oriented to the spiritual forces that rise from the earth. From the impression made by the eyes of the cow we can easily discern what her consciousness encompasses: she leads a dreaming existence in which she attends to the action of the earth's deep forces. Above all she feels herself connected with the sacred forces that continually rise up from the earth's interior. For us human beings these forces are not easy to grasp, but they manifest in the being and nature of the cow. Perceived supersensibly, the nature of the cow actually lies *within* the earth. The forces active in her are cosmic in nature but rather than radiating directly from above downward, they pass through the globe of the earth. The cosmic existence of the earth's interior becomes apparent in the being of the cow.

The unity which the cow has with the cosmos is apparent in her horns. The horns enable her to accomplish her earth-oriented mode of perception. Through them she is integrated into the cosmos as an earthly being, sustained by it and really enveloped. We can certainly see the cow as a messenger entering our world out of the inner, luminous, sacred existence of the earth.

What she accomplishes through her digestion tells us that her being serves the earth, right into earthly substance. In her dung becomes apparent how she is given up to the earth's renewal.

*

As human beings we possess an organ through which, like the cow, we belong to the earth: the solar plexus. Through the solar plexus the human individuality stands in a very particular soul and spiritual relationship to all surrounding processes. All processes of soul and spirit act upon and affect us through the solar plexus. Through it we are connected in soul and spirit with everything that happens in our environment. The solar plexus is an organ of hearing with which we hearken to the inner nature, the spiritual realities, of beings and things. The spiritual emanation of what occurs around us is always perceived by the solar plexus. The being or thing in question does not have to be physically present at all. What someone says or only thinks, for instance, moods and atmospheres, everything unspoken, is likewise perceived by the solar plexus.

The solar plexus is distinguished by its capacity to encompass the truth of a perception, a statement, a judgement. We can see it as an organ of truth. Through it we experience how true or untrue a comment or an action is. Thus the solar plexus is an organ of morality. It senses the depth of another being. Thanks to this organ we can develop a relationship with truthfulness or mendacity. It connects us with the spiritual world's sphere of truth. With it we can verify in the world of spirit how true something is that we encounter in the sense world.

Through the solar plexus the human being is committed to the truth of the earth in the same way that the cow, through her organism, is committed to the sacred light of the earth's interior. What the cow accomplishes at the level of substance through her organism, we accomplish at the soul and spiritual level with our solar plexus. Its yield is not dung—thus new, fertile earth—but sacred soul substance which, as it radiates, unfolds its healing effect in society. Truth heals, for it exerts no compulsion. The solar plexus is not an organ of power; it is far too bound up with the sacred powers of the cosmos for that. Every compulsion is at odds with the truth. Truth shows, represents but leaves free the person who acts.

*

Supersensible observation of the butterfly shows that it gathers around it a spiritual light that shines far out into the cosmos. Its lightness and weightlessness, its coloration, can show us that its meaning is not earthbound but relates to the cosmos. The butterfly only belongs to the earth in so far as it establishes a connection between the cosmos and the earth. It stands at the threshold between sense world and world of spirit. Through the light that is created as they flutter their wings, butterflies form a sphere that encompasses the whole earth. This sphere emits a special light that radiates outwards into the cosmos from the earth, creating a picture of the earth which appears in the cosmos. The beings of the angelic hierarchies behold the being of the earth in this light. They perceive the tasks of transformation which the earth organism has. They see how significant the earth is for the whole cosmos. The ascending butterfly light repeatedly calls upon the beings of the world of spirit to engage with the earth. They feel prompted to turn toward the life on earth. In the butterfly light appear the earth's gifts for the evolution of the cosmos. In it can be seen the grandiose work accomplished by human beings as they continually and repeatedly unite themselves with the earth organism.

In the light that ascends from butterflies into the world of spirit, the souls of human beings dwelling in the world of spirit find an essential orientation. They comprehend through it the meaning that connects them with the earth. They behold the sacred substance of earth existence that must be formed and increased. In the light of butterflies a significant truth does indeed live: the sphere appearing through the butterfly light invokes in unborn souls inner pictures that remind them of the sacred tasks that they have toward the earth, humanity and themselves.

*

In his passage through the world of earth, the Christ being also entered into a deep connection with animals. This may seem surprising at first glance, but following the event of Golgotha, Christ, like a wave, touches and penetrates the earth and all its creatures. The animals belong to the body of the earth; they are part of the earth organism, and for this reason it is their mission likewise to be bearers of the being of the resurrected Christ. Through the earth, the plants and minerals, through landscapes and through the animals, Christ looks upon the human being. His countenance shines in the depths of the beings and entities who inhabit the earth alongside us.

Just as Christ is a truth and reality in the world of rocks, plants and animals, so is he also for the beings of the elemental world. There are elemental beings who, when asked about their connection with Christ, wish to speak ceaselessly about how Christ lives amongst them, how he teaches and comforts them. They speak of how he came for the whole earth, of the fact that his lofty being has taken hold of the whole terrestrial existence of the earth. There is no place, no point anywhere on earth where he is not present. For the elemental beings he is the all-permeating, all-enlivening, all-transforming divine light. They are loyally devoted to him; in him they find the powers of cosmic continuance, and all the solace and support they need to continue their work despite the hindrances and resistance that come from humankind.

The animals are included in this healing and comforting gesture of the Christ being. They are bearers of his light, his power of transformation. If we consider the animals in close detail we find that they point to living aspects of the Christ being. He is always also in them. This can become apparent in the examples of the cow and the butterfly, which could easily be extended to other creatures as well. As we saw, cow and butterfly are the bearers of particular light qualities that testify to two very different aspects of Christ. Through cow nature shines the light of Christ that has deeply joined with the being of the earth and shines within it like a sun. The cow points us to where the earth has already become sun through coming in touch with the Christ being. For supersensible perception the earth transformed by Christ is already visible in the depths of the being of the cow. It shines almost unmistakeably through her eyes. Attentive observers will see this sacred light of the inner earth shining in a cow's eyes; they will feel themselves touched by the earth's already newborn future.

In polar contrast to this inner aspect of the living being of Christ represented by the cow, an enveloping light shines forth in the butterfly. The butterfly reveals the Christ being who appropriates the earth organism right out into the ensheathing, peripheral spheres that spread toward the cosmos. This is the Christ of the Ascension who has spread out over the whole earth organism. In the butterfly appears the Christ who guards the earth, envelops it, who is close to every living being and ensures that it retains his cosmic guardianship and thus also access to the world of spirit, to the region of spiritual archetypes.

*

We can gain the impression that the animals are standing amongst and with us; from a certain point of view this may be true, but from another they are ahead of us, above us, because, unlike us, they have never encountered the earth as separate beings. From the perspective of the animals, the human being is fallen since he lapsed from the ranks of Creation at the moment he developed self-consciousness. As human beings we can allow the animals to instruct us so that we can learn once more to belong fully to the earth thanks to the spiritual gifts we possess. The animals show us what it means to live in harmony with Mother Earth. But they can only become our exemplars and teachers in this if we learn to intuit, feel or perceive the spiritual depths of their nature. Only then do they reveal their true being to us. They are our teachers because they have never distanced themselves from the earth, unlike the human being who has done so by germinating powers of consciousness. The animals were sent to us to prevent us succumbing to the illusions to which we are exposed through this gift of self-awareness. They wish to heal us of all one-sidedness. Our centre is their holy aim. They stand by us so that we can evolve into a harmonious being, so that the opposing forces of life and existence unite within us. It is up to us to perceive and understand the gifts they possess by virtue of their deep connection with the Creation and the being of Christ.

15
The transformation of the soul, and the animals

The transformation of soul life signifies a great task for human beings. A person can only become an autonomous and free individuality by invoking the strength to order and govern their soul life by their own means, out of themselves. They are called upon to enter into a free relationship with their own soul being, their abilities, character traits, experiences, traumas and cavernous depths. Everyone has many aspects of their personality: the child, the anxious and the wise person, the fool, the fighter, and many more besides. We cannot avoid the task of bridging these different aspects. It can, however, prove a very arduous, wearisome labour to summon the tranquillity, certainty, will-power, sovereignty and trust that are necessary for this. Harmonizing and ordering soul faculties develop only slowly. We can even assume, with some comfort, that this work of transformation will extend over many lives. The Cypriot spiritual teacher Daskalos expresses this as follows:

> Gradually, lifetime by lifetime, a person learns to react less abruptly to irritations. All people are exposed to similar situations and circumstances. It is up to us how to understand and respond to every situation that arises: either with raging emotions or tranquil reason. [...] It is regrettable if humanity, numbed by matter and business, allows its consciousness to be formed by powers that act upon it—powers that result from more unedifying human emotions and desires. Consciousness has the authority and the will

to shape itself to be self-determining and not merely to be a plaything of time and circumstance.[9]

Daskalos speaks of a special source that we all bear within us and endows us with the capacity to act out of ourselves. This source is the living picture of our own higher being. Discovering this picture is a quest important for every single person in the world today. Even if we discover it only in rudimentary form, we are called upon to prove our mettle in life. In doing so we can rely on the efficacy of this picture, even if it does not always stand before our inner eye in full clarity. It is a picture we possess because we are beings of spirit whose whole scope is not fully revealed in earthly existence. In sleep, and still more in the period between death and rebirth, this picture inscribes itself deeply in the soul so that it is always possible for us to act out of it. John O'Donohue describes this process in the following words:

> It takes a long time to sift through the more superficial voices of your own gift in order to enter into the deep signature and tonality of your Otherness. When you speak from that deep, inner voice, you are really speaking from the unique tabernacle of your own presence. There is a voice within you that no one, not even you, has ever heard. Give yourself the opportunity of silence and begin to develop your listening in order to hear, deep within yourself, the music of your own spirit.[10]

We are not necessarily used to turning a loving attention toward our own high being, let alone forming a halfway faithful picture of this being. But it is helpful to call this picture to mind repeatedly, however vague and undefined it may be to begin with. We can try to conjure and paint it before our inner eye as a daily practice. But this will only work if we succeed in meeting ourselves without any value judgement. With continued practise of this exercise we can find that this work upon the image of our own essential being is indispensable for developing the strength and vigour we all need today to cope with life.

*

Supersensible observation shows that the animal beings work to transform human soul nature. The animals are accompanied from the world of spirit by high beings whom one could call the I of each animal. A single animal is not autonomous. It relates to its I in the world of spirit in the same way that a single cell relates to the whole organism. These high beings have a very particular relationship not only to the animal but to the human being as well. They surround us in a way that can be described as mediating to us essential gifts which we are not (or not yet) capable of bringing forth from ourselves. In this sense the human being is a child of the animals; they are our teachers. We are not yet mature enough for the mission that awaits us on earth. The animals hold us in our centre in a way that already mediates to us the capacities that we are still to develop.

This transformative work by the animals can be illustrated in the three examples below:

The deer is a creature that possesses a close affinity with a process whereby the Christ being, who historically appeared in earthly history, inscribes himself ever more deeply and clearly in earthly conditions. The being of the deer supports Christ's increasingly immanent presence in the earth. Even if this is not outwardly apparent, it bears the cosmic Christ in its antlers, serving him so that he becomes ever more deeply imprinted into the earth. For Christ the being of the deer is a portal through which he strides in order to be active within the life sphere of the earth, thus among human beings. The deer supports the process whereby the Christ becomes the life spirit of the earth. To do this the Christ must penetrate the substance and being of the earth, but also the creatures of the earth too. His life transforms into that of the earth, and that of the earth into his life. What is accomplished through the deer is a sacred occurrence. Like all antlered creatures, the deer is a very noble animal who, with its dreaming consciousness, gazes into the transformation process through which the life of the cosmos unites with the earth and gradually raises it to its future form. The antler-bearing creatures are fully immersed in this transformation process, safeguarding and nurturing it so that humankind can gradually take it over, step by step.

*

Study of the living reality of the bees shows that they are bearers of the image and thus also of the forces which the human soul must inwardly invoke in order to realize its future form. The wisdom of the hive points to capacities which we human beings will need for us to be equal to our future tasks. The wisdom of bees, manifest in every one of their life processes, is entirely cosmic in nature. Their life and existence is something we can only understand by using the soul faculties of Intuition. The secrets of the bees are interwoven with the awakening of intuitive perception in human beings. They are teachers of our higher evolution. Study of how they express their nature, and of how beekeepers relate to them, always refers us back to ourselves: bees summon us to behold ourselves, to perceive what of us and of our whole being we have already realized, and what still awaits realization.

The bees always also show us our shadow, our soul darkness. The varroa mite, which has affected the bees of many regions of the earth to such an extent that they are scarcely able to get over it without human aid, shows this very clearly. Through the varroa mite a shadow falls upon the bees that basically derives from humankind. The forces at work in the varroa are the same we summon in ourselves when we inwardly turn away from the living reality of the world of spirit. What tells us that a divine world cannot exist manifests in the life and reality of the bees. With varroa, bees take on something whose cause lies in the human being's stance toward the spirit. They reveal what the work of transformation would require for human beings to come to a true perception of earth's full reality. The shadows falling upon the bees are ones that have long been living in the human soul.

As beings of darkness and coldness, the varroa mites are nourished by the warmth and light of the bees, but in receiving this nourishment they inflict harm on the bees at the same time. They satisfy their longing to be healed by harming other creatures. It is the task of humankind to perceive these connections. Our response to the varroa mite is simply to annihilate it. But that is a useless attempt, and one in which we get no nearer to the root causes. True healing would involve transforming the shadows within *us* through the soul qualities of warmth and light; or, in other words, to bring our thinking and actions into harmonious accord with the living laws of the earth's spiritual reality. The varroa mite is a clear sign of the fact that a cure will not be found if we overlook the cause of suffering and only combat the effect or expression of it instead. It is not our task to combat the shadow and evil, all that is fallen or lapsed, but instead to raise what is fallen, to illumine the shadows and transform evil.

*

The snake is a creature that has a particular connection with the human being. It is our horizontal spinal column, raised in us into the vertical as the foundation for the evolution of human consciousness. The being of the snake exists in a field of tension between the spinal column's existence in a creature that crawls on the earth, and the function it fulfils in us. Each of us stands within this tension as soon as we enter into an individual relationship with the world of spirit. We can choose what we do, how we conduct ourselves, which worldview we adopt, what we think, which ideas we subscribe to. This freedom of choice is a gift of the snake. It gives itself up to the earth when it crawls on the ground; but it also gives itself to us when we seek our own intrinsic position and perspective, when we strive to fulfil our tasks, to express our true being. The snake embodies in the earthly realm an image that can show us what the work of redemption involves, how it can come to fruition for the earth and for all creatures—for the snake desires its own redemption. Through the snake the human being raises himself. What humankind accomplishes for the snake is the picture of a process which, related to the entirety of the earth, has not yet been concluded. In relation to the whole earth we bear the same responsibility as we do toward the being of the snake. If we had not raised the snake we would not be what we are. We will not become what we are destined to be without absorbing and internalizing the whole earth, as we have done the snake.

*

Without being aware of it, the human being receives—or conceives—the lofty work of the animals in every moment of life. We do this whenever we become aware of what we ourselves can already accomplish. By valuing and accepting who we have already become we accept the secret work of animals. We have gained many valuable experiences through the life we have already lived on earth. We have previously lived in many different eras of human evolution, thereby acquiring significant capacities. By affirming this life-stream we connect with the whole earth, thus also with the gifts granted us by the animals. We will be able to feel how the animals have long accompanied us, through all the lives we have lived. They play an important part in our lives. The work of transformation of the earth accomplished by the animals has made us what we are; it is only by virtue of ourselves that we are what we are. The high animal beings are the bearers of human evolution. To them we owe our inner strength, our powers of soul, the multiplicity of our soul life. As we evolve we always do so *with* the animals. We owe what we are to the fact that they are our siblings.

*

The terrestrial life of animals does not necessarily manifest the deep and inherent connection that exists between the world of animals and the human being. Their mode of life within earthly conditions does, certainly, allow us to sense their spiritual character and spiritual tasks, but we will only be able to grasp these fully if we turn with discernment to their respective spirit beings. The spirit beings of animals have a deep relationship with the human being's cosmic nature. The animal beings have the lofty task of enabling human beings to develop their soul nature in such a way that they can take Christ into them. From the cosmos, the spirit beings of animals mantle our human soul nature such that we become able to maintain a harmonious and balanced relationship with it. The animals support us in enhancing our soul and thus developing the powers to engage ever more deeply with the being of Christ. The spirit beings of the animals are guardians of the human soul's high and most elevated capacities. They embody spiritual portals for gifts through which the human soul can feel nourished, sustained, invigorated and ultimately comforted. Through these spirit beings humankind is ennobled, elevated and strengthened.

When we turn inwardly to the animals, we will feel and discern how close they are to us and what redemptive, liberating and harmonizing impulses pass to us through them. Indeed, we can speak of a stream of animal spirit beings flowing into us. To open ourselves to this stream means taking a great step in the connection and relationship between animal and human existence.

*

The Christ being's work seeks to maintain every human being's capacity to develop the rudiments of their higher self in freedom. As from the lofty animal beings, no compelling influence proceeds from him. If this were not so, we could not develop our potential. Christ does not prescribe to us what we must do, but he wants us to decide which direction we turn in and which star we follow. Christ prepares us for this in so far as we perceive the consequences of our actions. All compulsion and thus also all punishment is foreign to Christ's nature. He is a divine being whose hands are tied, who relinquishes the exercise of power because that would contradict our evolution toward freedom. The impulse of the Christ being is one thoroughly wedded to freedom. Each person is completely and unconditionally free to turn toward the Christ being or not. It is up to us to take these steps or to omit to take them. An unfree decision runs counter to the essential nature of Christ.

16
The path to birth

As human beings we feel our way tentatively toward life's reality.
Its meaning is not always easy to grasp. But being tentative also means being careful. Taking things slowly means being more thorough. Discernment of the essential nature of our own destiny and tasks in life sometimes only gleams before us like a will-o'-the-wisp and then is lost again in darkness. Any greater vision or insight often comes unexpectedly and unrepeatably, revealing with sudden, surprising clarity the source from which our own destiny rises day after day. Usually such insight rises from an inchoate realm: for a moment one has the certainty of a higher mission that justifies and explains one's own existence. The clarity fades, and looking back later we may perhaps only be sure *that* we knew at that moment. A certainty remains that we were touched by what is at once the wisdom and childlike nature of our own being.

*

We are sensing something that seems much greater and more expansive than we presently are. Just as the earth only reveals a part of her comprehensive being to sense observation, so we do not yet behold our entirety. Now the earth, the creatures who dwell upon her, the events of destiny, are there to lead us toward ourselves. Our own life is the best example of how the earth does not let us go, how she keeps faith with us, letting day follow night, spring follow winter, high tide follow low tide—with an exactitude that can deeply affect us, that can give rise to wonder at the care, the lawfulness, the security she gives us. The earth is precise, lawful, in a way that is deeply awe-inspiring; and yet we still have the scope and freedom to live our own life, express our inherent nature.

*

Being born is a lifelong process. This is because our scope of freedom arises *through* the earth herself. We experience freedom through the earth, through what she gives us at every moment of our lives. Is that why we seek the earth? Is the freedom she makes possible for us the reason we unite with her, love her—to such a degree that we return here life after life?

The freedom to make our own decisions is indeed a potential capacity which represents a remarkable contrast to the general laws discernible in the earthly realm. We can make mistakes, errors, which are the shadow-side of freedom. Among the creatures that dwell upon earth alongside us we find none that can err as we do: they are pervaded by a wisdom which we, as beings of soul endowed with consciousness do not easily have available to us. But that is what we seek as human beings on earth: the scope for development. The fact that we do not possess the wisdom of plants and animals, of the planet as a whole, is painful; but on the other hand it is this that gives us the free scope which other creatures do not have. In the interplay between law and freedom, between necessity and free choice, the human being incarnates on earth. We seek these polarities, which are necessary to us.

*

At the same time this also describes the chief tasks that the beings of the elemental world have in relation to the human being. The human soul incarnates into this realm of freedom when it comes from pre-birth existence. It is the elemental beings who create this realm, which enables human beings gradually to feel their way through the most varied circumstances and express their being. But the elementals do not create this out of themselves; they do so together with the higher beings of the world of spirit, primarily with the blessed powers that come from the being of Christ and penetrate their world. We must picture this as an ongoing, ceaseless life-stream that flows to the beings of the elemental world from the Christ being. Christ implants in the world of elemental beings something that is reflected in human life as the capacity to make free decisions. Our freedom of choice is an actual reality in the elemental world—if this were not so it would not be available to us in our soul and spirit.

*

Our physical birth from a mother is preceded by the birth of the soul from the earth. The soul does not fall from the heavens into the mother's body but is first received by the being of the earth. Our bodily mother is the second being to take up the human germ once the earth organism, the Earth Mother, has previously done so. Within her the cosmic being of the unborn soul unites with its forthcoming earthly destiny. The earth organism provides the soul with the surety that the destiny that was interrupted at the last death can find its continuation. The soul's longing to be able to continue its destiny is satisfied—its heavenly wanderings come to an end.

*

Between earthly incarnations the soul is accompanied by a luminosity originating from the earth and radiating through the cosmos. During its journey through supersensible worlds, the soul takes its orientation from this light. What happens on this journey is always connected with the earth, which remains central for dead and unborn souls, a pillar that enables them to find their bearings.

On its journey toward a bodily mother, the soul migrates through the spiritual strata of the earth—in other words, the planetary spheres encompassing the earth in living sheaths. In the lowest sphere, the moon sphere, the soul encounters beings who already have their dwelling on earth. They too lead and guide it, and during this period it absorbs the wisdom of beings belonging to the elemental kingdom. These beings have a special closeness with unborn souls and implant in them the capacities for essential qualities that become apparent later in life in, among other things, the gifts of listening and intuitive understanding. If someone has a close relationship with the elemental world, it can be assumed that they were already taught by these beings during their pre-birth existence. These are human souls whose previous lives have endowed them with qualities that are important and significant for the elemental beings especially.

*

The mother receives the soul through her crown chakra. The human being's supersensible crown is the fitting spiritual organ for receiving unborn souls. The unborn soul that has already been received or conceived by the earth organism finds through its parents the possibility of developing a corporeality that will serve it in a forthcoming life on earth.

Before the soul is received by its mother, it has a perception of the parent couple. It may also have several sets of parents in view, or may even land very unexpectedly with a mother who only slept once with a man whom she scarcely knew. The choice the soul makes is not always ideal. From a higher perspective this does not even matter. It can be far more important for the soul to pursue a path which eventually leads to acquiring an earthly body. The historical conditions, the political and social circumstances in a particular country, the character of a people, the nature of a city or landscape, can be far more decisive for the soul's development than the couple to whom it comes. Or it may simply seize a particular opportunity since time is pressing, or another person or group is drawing it to a particular place, or because the experiences the soul needs are only possible in this region.

Nevertheless, what lives between the couple as mutual affection, respect and love is important and formative for the soul, endowing it with essential inner qualities such as trust, security and a sense of self-worth. If this can happen, the soul will not have to battle so hard in its forthcoming life to acquire these qualities. Otherwise a person will need to develop such qualities by their own efforts. But this can also be the very task the soul has set itself—to develop through its own work, under earthly conditions, what it has not received from its parents.

*

As a person incarnates they also seek the experience of pain, an important teacher that has an awakening effect of great value for the further development of an individuality. Privation, loneliness, disappointments are essential experiences without which a person cannot develop. This is why we experience pain arising from our own destiny. It may begin at a very early stage, already before birth. Pain only appears unpleasant, onerous or even terrible when we live on earth. Seen from the world of spirit, experiences of pain are the germ for a path of development that sometimes reaches far into the future, a sowing of seeds that do not immediately grow. Through pain something in the future is prepared which, in our present life, we are as yet too little able to accept or appreciate. Its fruits will only become fully visible after one or even several passages between earthly lives. The maturity to accept the grace that lies in pain is something we still need to develop.

The highest gods concern themselves with the pain of a human being. Reaching far up into the cosmos, its rays are transformed into gentle love that returns to the soul to become its possession and endowment. This may only happen after death. No human pain remains unanswered by the grace of the angels. We are too much children of the cosmos to be left, in our pain, to ourselves alone.

17
Paths into life

Do I know my own foundations? It is clear that I stand through my own powers—I do not stand upright by clinging to another. I bear within me the wellspring out of which I act, day after day. I myself am that source.

But what does this I of mine comprise? It disappears into a boundless realm. It rises from who knows where. It is equally unclear where it is heading and what will become of it. The I resists consciousness, outshining it. Its light comes from a boundless beyond. Consciousness has no means, nor concepts, for grasping the nature of the I. At the same time the I is very close, in fact extraordinarily close. After all I only exist by virtue of this I; and yet it is without beginning—its source and origin elude me.

There is no doubt that something unmistakeably unique is present on the earth with every human being: an inimitable power, a quality, a living being works through each of us. Each person experiences themselves as unique. There are no two identical individualities on earth.

*

Inherent in the I is an overwhelming innocence. It exists without demands; a power issues from it devoid of all wish for dominance; it lends uprightness, but without any egotism. From it shines a light that lives within it alone; nevertheless it is fleeting and withdraws, flees, if it is denied space, recognition, esteem. It is apparent that we are only slowly coming to know ourselves, that we are on a journey toward ourselves.

*

The power of individuality inherent in each person eludes our concepts. We discern it only on the far side of all thoughts. It is fitting therefore that at particular moments we become foreign to ourselves, and meet our own I as if it were another, a stranger. In other words, we continually become newly acquainted with ourselves. We are never the one we think we are. We have many aspects. So far we know only a very few of them, for they are still in the process of becoming.

*

The I is the name I give myself. But it is more: it is the strength from which my individuality proceeds; and still more: the being within which my higher being, my divine self, comes to expression. By nature we are beings of spirit, gods really. In the I, this entity that for us is dual and divided—both fleeting and powerful—our divine nature reveals itself. The symbolic language of our I is that of a divine being.

The I, our divine name, is kindled during life in response to the earth. In sleep or after death it is received by our higher self in the spiritual world. The higher self is our divine nature, something we are from the very beginning of our existence *as well as* what we are still to become. During earthly life, the higher self does not live in its perfect and complete form in the I. We do not yet have the maturity to enable our self to be fully present in earthly conditions. In forthcoming eras of evolution, we will become able to bear our higher self into earthly existence with ever greater clarity and power.

*

The higher self hearkens to the wisdom and laws of the divine world. It has no need to bind itself to what is untrue or mistaken. To open to it means experiencing oneself as a being whose source lies in the world of spirit. From the physical world we receive our bodily sheaths. We are born there, live our life, and, when we die, depart from these physical sheaths in order to unite with our higher being in the world of spirit. After death we unite with our higher being and all Creation. There we receive what the earth will gain through us and our destiny during our subsequent life upon it. We receive our gifts, the love that carries us through life, the devotion with which we observe things, the fullness out of which we feel and the strength of our will.

*

We never cease to be the cosmic child we are from earliest beginnings. Earthly life may afflict us, may seek to use all means to rob us of our right to existence, may extinguish our memories of this child. But she retains her strength for she is cosmic and inextinguishable. As human beings we remain children of the cosmos. The streams that connect us with the cosmos may be invisible but they are also unquenchable.

We never lose our connection with our higher being. But we do distance ourselves from it in order to fulfil our earthly tasks. If this were not so, we would remain the fully divine self that we originally are, and could never inhabit a physical body. The human self, our perfect, divine being, is filled with cosmic life. It has its source in divine existence. Its home is the cosmos. We can only lead our life on earth when what we call our I detaches itself from our greater self. The human I is a child of the self, endowed with its own life.

Daskalos (Stylianos Atteshlis), the Cypriot spiritual teacher, expresses this as follows: 'The selfhood of each of us [...] remains in a state of unity with absolute beingness, but extends downward to our often struggling present personality.'[11]

*

In the world of spirit between different lives on earth, we live in harmony with our higher self. This self is united with the cosmos just as the I is united with the earthly world during life. Through our higher self the cosmos becomes a reality for us, just as the earthly world becomes a reality through our I. During life on earth a person usually loses all memory of their higher self's pre-birth existence. The experiences we have gained through our earthly I are integrated during our existence in the spiritual world into our experiences of lives previously lived. We experience these lives like pupae, as states of being we once inhabited. In the same way we can behold forthcoming lives as seeds whose intrinsic nature is as yet concealed from us.

In our successive lives we work at developing our individuality. Because, as a part of humanity, it is our task to enter into a deep connection with the being of the earth, we are exposed to the influence of the forces that have led the earth to the level of matter. We must engage with these forces during our lives on earth. Thus working on our I also always means working on the earth and on the forces that have hitherto brought it into a material condition. But these are forces described as being the source of evil in the world. As we stand up to them, wrestle with them, we work to develop our individuality to a higher condition. By this means it accrues powers that could not be gained anywhere else in the cosmos.

*

The karma that awaits a person on earth affects the form in which their I will manifest in this present life. Karma comprises the tasks a person must undertake according to the nature of their actions in previous lives. In fulfilling these tasks we have to redeem our previous culpable conduct, something that can only be done by the person who took those past actions. In the period between two lives, a person perceives the need for redressing or balancing their karma on the earth, which is itself a reason for wishing to unite with the earth once again. We will enter into a life and life situations that will serve us to transform our karma. What appears during our life to be misfortune, suffering, sorrow, will in many cases be meaningful opportunities for redressing karmic debts.

Depending on the way in which the earthly being of a person, thus their individuality, is constituted, they will have the means to transform their karma. During life on earth our I exists in a form that is neither identical with our higher self, nor is it identical with the forms that each I possessed in our previous lives, since each served different aspects of the work of transformation of our being.

It is therefore mistaken to extrapolate our identity solely from what we experience as our earthly I, for it is only a part of the higher self out of which this I being emerged to enable us to live out our present, very particular biography. Our inner being shines into worlds of spirit, from where the I receives its higher guidance. As soon as we identify only with our earthly biography we grasp a part of our true being, certainly, but at the same time limit it because we fail to discern the entirety of our spiritual essence.

*

The higher self is the source of love. When we truly love we raise ourselves to our highest nature. But love does not release us from distress. Those who love simply come to know a different aspect of distress, for the power of love reveals precisely what does not stand in the light of truth. It makes shadows visible in a way not easily endured by someone who does not know how to protect themselves. Those who love follow the path of truth. They look lies in the face, the reality of shadows and evil, and will need to develop strategies for coping with this. Love reveals all colours of reality, including wayward and dark ones. It is a sign of love to despair at lies, including those we ourselves are still chained to. Love is not only a strengthening power, it also consumes the soul and can weaken it; which is why it is not enough to develop love only. It is also essential that we strengthen ourselves. It takes soul strength to love; alongside surrender and devotion we need the strength of self-assertion, of certainty and stability. Otherwise love only binds anew the one who practises it rather than liberating them.

*

A person's biography is a living picture of the individuality at work within earthly conditions. We can read this picture if we grasp the various events in a biography as fragments of the mirror in which, when taken as a whole, a person's being becomes manifest. In each of these fragments—since it is part of the living whole (of a living picture)—lies the possibility of grasping the whole. But to do so a special power is needed: precise imagination. The whole being is always present in each separate or succeeding picture. It never loses its connection with the whole, just as a flowering plant always already bears seed and fruit within it, for otherwise it would possess no life. Since the whole plant is always contained in the seed, albeit spiritually, development has an aim and orientation. In exactly the same way each separate picture and occurrence, every experience, belongs to our destiny. Nothing is random.

*

We can now begin to compile the pictures of our own life. To do so we turn our inner gaze to the panorama of our life hitherto, observing its many events and experiences which together form our biography. Our own life stands before us, and we can now feel a need to appropriate and integrate these pictures in a new way. They have occurred but do not all belong to us in the same way. There will be a series of occurrences from which we keep a greater distance because we have not yet reconciled ourselves with them. Inner, intentional work will be needed to own these experiences. They resist this, and usually we will not succeed at the first attempt. Toward certain actions we feel shame, wishing they had not been, and we push them away from us as if they were not part of the whole. But they are. Or we wish we had had a different childhood, other abilities; we wish life had taken a different course. But these unfulfilled aspects are also part of our individuality, belong to it just as much as our successes, moments of happiness, and experiences that have given deep pleasure and satisfaction.

Consciously gathering together the whole panorama of our life is a quiet and lovely labour: we can feel that we only enter into a true relationship with ourselves when we succeed in turning toward our own shadow, toward what is profoundly contradictory in us, with an inner gesture of affirmation. Now the contradictions are nothing other than a part of our own light. Only when we place the shadows into the light of our own attention will they brighten. For this we have to accept them. Only when we do so can the unfulfilled aspects of our being, the unhappiness, the pain we have suffered or have caused, be led back to their true purpose—that is, to teach us. Inner growth can be practised especially in relation to what has remained unfulfilled and unredeemed. The great hidden being we always also are is concealed in the events of our lives: comprising all colours, it is strong enough to bear even the deepest darknesses—despair, pain, depression, fear. The higher self is especially alive in these since they contain the greatest possibilities of transformation.

*

An inner strength is certainly needed to endure what happens when I give myself up to the pictures of my life. It can easily happen that I am overwhelmed by the reliving of memories, the triggering of flash-backs difficult to cope with. Then I plunge back into experiences against which I have so far been able to defend myself: sad, humiliating, fear-inducing experiences hurt me all over again. We can only meet them without being injured if we are strong enough.

If we feel too weak, it is better to let sleeping dogs lie. If we want to encounter them without succumbing to their shadows all over again, for a second, third or even fourth time, we will need access to the wellsprings of our own strength. It is important to know: *Where does my strength lie?* It may be an ability of mine, a talent, a place in my body, a place in the landscape, a memory, a particular person whom I make contact with, either actually or in imagination, so as to assure myself of my intrinsic strength. Only in this way can I survive in the face of things, when I encounter them again, that I had to defend myself against before.

18

Death as a doorway into new existence

The earth is solid and impenetrable in so far as we are beings pos-sessing a physical body. The physical body can only be phys-ically united with the earth. It can move over and across it, clamber into caves or climb mountains. The earth remains hard substance for the physical body, but impermeable to it. But for us as beings of soul and spirit, it is anything other than impenetrable. With the powers of our soul and spirit we can give ourselves over to the world of phenom-ena and will then come to experiences that reveal the earth as a living and soul-pervaded being.

The soul can penetrate what the senses perceive as solid, hard and sensory earth. The soul is not bound to the phys-ical world in the way the physical body is: it can enlarge and expand, and thus delve beyond the realm that rep-resents an insuperable barrier for the physical body. The soul is softer and more delicate than the physical body. It can intentionally and unintentionally connect with a soul substance underlying what we call the physical world. This is impossible for the senses: they are repulsed by the fur-ther strata of reality lying beneath the surface of the phys-ical world. The soul, though, can immerse itself in them, can empathize and unite with what is inaccessible to the senses. Actually we have many such experiences through which the soul connects with what appears to us as the sensory and solidly fashioned world. Indeed, we could not really exist at all if we did not possess these capacities. But our consciousness is not sufficiently schooled, not attentive enough to notice that our soul directly crosses the threshold of sense existence. Really we are always living also in what is called the 'beyond', which is in fact only and profoundly the present and immanent.

*

Observed more precisely, every sense perception is a supersensible occurrence. In every sense perception we grow together with the objects of our gaze, uniting with them. If we attend more carefully to what is happening in every sense perception, we discover that our higher being, which eludes mere sensory observation, intimately resonates with the reality of being that imparts itself in every sense perception.

Even the mere shape of a leaf, the movement of an animal, a human voice, deeply inscribes itself in the soul. The same is true of everything. There is nothing ultimately hidden from our being of soul, which resonates in concord with every perception. The sense impressions elicited for example when we meet another person, make their way through our own soul being, migrate through the soul. Experiences we have are assimilated in us, digested if you like, thus become an incalculable part of our being. They leave traces in us. Within us lives not only the sense nature of our perceptions but also the deeper essence of every occurrence.

*

Death reveals its secrets if, in full waking consciousness, we allow what happens with someone when they die to happen to us. By becoming able consciously to cross the threshold which death signifies for human experience, we can gain glimpses into the world of the dead. Then we discern that the soul after death passes through important processes of transformation.

Anyone who has experienced the pain of taking leave of someone when they die, yet at the same time attentively observes what occurs in their connection with that person in the following period, which can last years, will be able to gain experiences that confirm a further existence after death. The dead person does not simply vanish. Death is a physical reality, but also one of soul and spirit. The dead give utterance, which we can receive if we are attentive to what happens to and around us. The dead remain connected with those they love.

Death separates two conditions of the soul's existence that could not be more different from each other. It signifies something completely different for someone living in a physical body than for the one who has died. To a view of things focused exclusively on sense reality, death is an impenetrable boundary and an insoluble enigma. But since, for the person overtaken by death, it signifies a crossing of the threshold, we can only fully comprehend their being by discerning this crossing and accompanying it.

The dead soul finds itself in a condition in which, as a rule, what is happening among people it knew in life is not hidden from its perception. The view from beyond the threshold is much easier than it is from this side. It is a perfectly normal part of the life of the dead to be connected with the living.

*

The bond between the dead and those living within earthly conditions is unbreakable. The dead retain interest in the people with whom they lived on earth, and, as far as possible, help serve their development. That this is possible signifies a great relief for them since, now they have left their earthly body behind, they can support these people in a way that was not possible during life. They can intervene deeply in their destiny by acknowledging, from their perspective, the wishes of those people they seek to support. In the world they have now entered, they do not know jealousy but are relieved when the person with whom they were connected discovers and develops in themselves something the dead person obstructed when living with them. The dead are soothed and comforted when people they left behind are able to make developmental steps only possible now, after they have left them.

Every relationship which people have on earth results in those involved in it developing in a certain direction, and at the same time this means that other directions are not pursued. It is perfectly natural that every human relationship both enlarges *and* restricts possibilities.

After death, the person also beholds the aspects of development which their partner was unable to express and realize when they lived together. This gives rise to the need to make good such lack, and the soul supports their partner in doing so as far as they are able. If the partner left behind was prevented during a marriage from fulfilling a deep wish they had, the one who has died will seek its fulfilment to the degree they are able. It can also be observed that the dead help lead the husband or wife left behind to people who can redress the influence that they themselves exercised on their partner during life.

*

The dead person, however, also desires to progress in things they were unable to realize during life. In the panorama of life unfolding after death, the soul perceives the degree to which it has actually realized what lay within its potential. The soul beholds what it has omitted to do, what remained unfulfilled due to mistaken decisions, weakness or simply through unfortunate circumstances. It tries to convey to people with whom it lived during life the impulses—which they can either assimilate or not—that were unable to become reality. It might be that a person shied away from becoming a doctor even though they could have become a very good one, and now supports a grandchild in studying medicine. Or they might try to prevent their daughter and husband, say, from making the same mistakes in marriage that they themselves made with their partner. Possible instances are too numerous to mention. But if we look attentively at what happens in human biographies, each of us may well find examples that illustrate how the life impulses of the dead pass to those still living.

All this sheds a light on the streams of destiny flowing between the world of the living and of the dead. But taking on the unlived destiny of another person who has died should never restrict our own freedom. Rather, it should serve our own development, broadening, encouraging and strengthening us, and never weakening and limiting our own powers. It is therefore good to practise caution if you feel that you are connected with the dead. You should not shy away from such connection but nor should you lose sight of the fact that it must help you to live your life out of the intrinsic sources and depths of your own being.

19

Death as the source of life

Death is the birth of the soul in another world. After death the soul enters a world that is entirely different from the one in which it has previously lived. It accomplishes a transition that leads it into a quite different form of existence. The soul that has just left the body is received by the beings of the other world in a way that can make it seem as if it has not died at all. Life immediately continues. Death is a transition, a transformation that does not affect the soul's inmost core, its essential being. Its inherent and intrinsic nature is not lost. It passes into another world, but one that changes nothing in the deep content of its own essence.

In fact, after the soul has laid aside the physical body and left it behind, another body is given it from the world of spirit. This spirit body surrounds the soul and makes it a part of the spiritual world just as the physical body made it a part of the physical world. We can picture this spirit body as an organ which now connects the soul with the spiritual world, enabling it to find its way in this world, to move around and enter into connection with the beings who dwell there. The soul experiences this body as the precondition for its rebirth in the world into which it has been transposed by death. The spirit body contains all the experiences the soul has had during its previous lives on earth. It encompasses the greater self with all earthly experiences it has so far acquired, thus the essence of all its lives on earth. At this moment the soul experiences the totality underlying its being: the grandeur, perfection and multiplicity of its entire being comes to its awareness. It feels how it owes this being to all its previous lives; but also to the spiritual contexts and beings which it now meets after death. Only they, in fact, are able to make the whole human being cohere. The soul who has died experiences itself as a part of this greater human being, who can only exist by being kept safe by the spirit world and the lofty beings who dwell there. This greater human being is the source and origin of the soul living on earth, to which it returns again after death.

*

Nothing of what we experience on earth is lost. Into the spirit body we receive after death are inscribed all the experiences of all our previous lives. These are the foundation of our further journey through spirit worlds, which eventually leads to us being incarnated again on earth. The soul gains an awareness of how earthly lives adhere to a certain lawfulness, originating with the high beings of the world of spirit. It is the cosmic order which, depending on our deeds in previous lives, establishes and shapes our future destiny.

*

After death the person who has died beholds their last life. This life panorama is of great significance for through it we can look upon our life from a higher perspective. To find this perspective in earthly life is only possible by developing special moral powers. After death the soul beholds the deeds of its previous life in resonance with a higher moral judgement that originates not from itself but from the world of spirit. Our deeds are measured against a higher standard. We behold our own life as that of another. This gaze causes us shame on the one hand, for it unveils our frailties, ill deeds and errors; but we also look upon the many positive influences that have proceeded from us, of which we may have had no inkling previously. This life panorama, through which after death we gain a new, higher standpoint towards ourselves, is accompanied by the being of Christ. Christ enables the soul that has separated from its earthly body to gain this broader view of its previous life. This special vision is subject to his influence. The dead person, however, will not inevitably recognize this influence. Whether or not they do so is connected with the ideas they have formed in their life on earth of the nature and being of Christ. In a sense the soul now looks with the eyes of Christ. This gaze is very redemptive and liberating, for through it a great longing is quenched: finally to see ourselves in a true light.

During this panorama, the person who has died also perceives the deeds of theirs that have incurred culpability, but at the same time feels accompanied by the gentleness and faithfulness of Christ. Because of this they become aware of how Christ takes human culpability upon himself. We feel our guilt but equally feel unconditionally accepted by Christ, who will stand by us as we expunge our guilt. There is no need to feel abandoned by Christ because we have burdened ourselves with guilt. This does not mean, though, that we bear no responsibility for the immoral deeds we have done. We discover that Christ will stand by us when, in a future life, we seek to redress these deeds. No kind of guilt degrades a person in the gaze of Christ. He never turns his loving gaze away from the essence of a person's being. We learn after death how Christ always accepts us. We learn that nothing in the world can be strong enough to sunder us from the love of the Christ being.

*

For the soul to be received into the world of spirit, it must pass through a process of cleansing in the life after death. It releases itself from everything originating in its earthly life that would cause resistance to life in the world of spirit. Not everything a person has done, felt and thought during life on earth is suited to enabling their soul to unite with the beings of the spirit world. To prepare its life in this world, the soul must be freed from these hindrances. It is a matter here of the soul shedding the qualities and habits that have bound it to earthly life to an excessive degree. Someone who has invested a great deal in sensory existence will take longer to be cleansed than someone who has lived in a modest and frugal way. But they will also take longer to free themselves if they have bound themselves to certain over-fixed ideas or views, from which, likewise they will need to detach themselves before they can journey further.

*

The moment of death retains a great significance for the soul throughout its whole after-death path. It repeatedly looks back on it as a point of orientation through which it feels how, despite its present spiritual existence, it remains connected with the earth. On its journey toward its next incarnation, the soul never loses this connection with the earth. Earth existence remains the focus of all that the soul experiences in the world of spirit. The dead person's attention is turned toward life on earth; its connection with the earth never ceases during its spiritual sojourn.

The moment of death has a further significance too. It is the moment when the soul for the first time turns its gaze to the true connection between the world of earth and the world of spirit. It awakens in the spiritual world and discerns that the physical world could not exist without the spiritual world, and that the soul itself inherently and originally belongs to the spiritual world.

After death we behold and experience our true being, which can be very different from what we thought it to be during our earthly life. We discover that we succumbed to misjudgements, misinterpretations and mistakes in pursuing our life's goals. Such insight may be painful but is balanced by the certainty that we will go on weaving our life's thread. As we make our way through the spiritual world, we gain the maturity and ability to take new hold of our development and progress onwards with it from the point at which we stood at our last death.

*

The dead are intimately connected with those living on earth. They participate in what people do on earth because they know the great value of the earth and life on earth for all development. They do all in their power to support the living, but are also dependent on receiving the support of the living. The thoughts, feelings or will impulses of the living are certainly perceived by the dead. If consciously turned toward them, they are an important wellspring for them. Thoughts we send them, rites and rituals we arrange for them, actions we carry out in their name, are a great help to them. It is an unforgettable moment for one who has died to feel that a living person really opens to them, thus seeks to be connected with them. This closes a circle that had been ruptured at death, though such rupture has no reality from the perspective of the dead. At such moments the dead person feels deeply moved, accepted and sustained by those living on earth. Their connection with the earth, for which they feel intense love, is thereby renewed in a way that gives them strength and confidence. Those who need a long time to release themselves from earthly ties are especially reliant on this support.

People living on earth can feel the closeness of the dead soul they have known especially when they perform actions that this soul liked to perform. This might be very mundane actions such as washing up or gardening. The dead retain a strong connection with things they themselves enjoyed doing. When one of those they have left behind carries out such an action, they are drawn to it and can share in it from their world, in this way connecting with the earth and those they have loved. It is important to pay heed to the fact that the dead still feel a longing for the earth and life on earth.

It is also important to note that in our converse with the dead we should always practise care and caution, especially when the cleansing of their soul requires great work and effort. Such work of transformation is laborious and hard and puts the dead soul in a state that is hard to endure, and sometimes even tormenting for them. They are deprived of the people with whom they shared their life, and seek their support. This can sometimes mean that those still alive feel compelled to actions that were previously alien to them. They feel an inclination to adopt certain habits of the dead person. For the latter this signifies an easing of their suffering but for those still alive it can lead to very unpleasant states. A sense can arise for them of no longer properly inhabiting themselves. Great care must be taken here. We have the right and duty to reject a dead person's desire before it exceeds our own capacities to cope with it. This is something that must definitely be remembered. It is advisable to ensure that we have the protection of the world of spirit when we notice that we have become involved in this work of post-mortem transformation. Prayers, verses and meditations offer a means to protect ourselves.

*

There is a bond between people living on earth and in the worlds of spirit. The ascending and descending human souls work upon the connection between these worlds, between earth existence and the cosmos. What happens between the worlds, thus between the dead, unborn human souls and those living within earthly conditions, is of great importance for this connection. Every time we think of the world of the dead and unborn souls, this bond is strengthened. It is very sustaining, giving souls trust and confidence, reconciling, calming and strengthening them. This bond is strengthened when people living on earth work consciously with it. It cannot be left to itself but requires our attention. By the power of consciousness kindled through earthly life and conditions, it can be decisively enhanced. Ultimately a bond of peace is formed in this way and becomes ever more resilient. By means of it earth and cosmos come closer to each other: the worlds grow together, something of great importance for the future of the earth and humanity. This bond can be experienced as a spiritual vessel receiving from the beings of the cosmos powers of futurity that the earth needs for its further evolution.

20

The relationship of the dead with the earth and human beings

We can ask how a dead soul experiences the earth. How are they connected with earth's realities despite laying the body aside? How do they regard the earth and to what extent do they affect it? If we address these questions from the perspective of supersensible research, it becomes apparent that, after death, earth existence acquires a special value. During life on earth this is our self-evident domain. After death we look upon the earth with a sense of great reverence for the life we led there, and will one day lead again.

Earthly existence acquires a special value for the dead, for then we no longer regard it from without, that is, through its sensory surface. We are deprived of our senses, and instead we behold the earth spiritually, possessing an inner gaze of the earth's nature and being. Now, from the world of spirit, we no longer look *upon* life's phenomena but *out* of them, from within them. We now look outwards from what, during life, we looked upon from without, thus with our senses. If, during life, we have, say, concerned ourselves with crystals, have perhaps collected them, maybe even traded in them, we now experience them from within.

Then also we rediscover ourselves within the things and beings that preoccupied us, in such a way that we *experience ourselves through these things and beings*. Through a crystal itself we experience how we related to it in our previous life. We behold the interaction or relationship we cultivated with things. Thus through these things and beings we come to self-knowledge. This can relate to everything that we did on earth, and all that we fashioned or created. If we worked as a gardener, we gain inner experience of the plants with which we engaged. We feel the nature of these plants but also the way in which we cultivated them, the degree of devotion and attentiveness we brought to this work. If we worked in a caring profession and as a therapist, we experience ourselves through the people we nursed and treated. The same is true of everything. After death we come to an inner view of the entities and creatures that played an important part in our previous life, and this leads to deep experiences of our connection with the earth. We feel the spiritual reality of stones, plants, animals. We perceive how the world of spirit participates in their living existence, and discern at first hand the spiritual connections at work in everything and everyone.

*

The dead person now lives inwardly in those they were close to during their past life. From time to time they will actually indwell them. Their body has decayed and become inaccessible, but the soul can slip into another human body. This is a very welcome opportunity for a dead person, for it allows them to come a little closer to earthly existence once more. Sensitive people will feel when a dead soul approaches them. Usually this occurs only for a short while, and is a lovely experience for the person in question, for then we will feel ourselves close to a beloved one who has departed. We may feel prompted to carry out an action that the dead person loved to do, or will recall experiences we had with them. We may also feel the stirring of particular impulses that are important for our destiny. An idea will germinate in us that can be important for our further life. Or a feeling surfaces that we can be content with what we have so far accomplished. It may also be that we simply feel relaxed, light-hearted and happy.

The dead are able to support the people with whom they were connected during life. They can stand by them in difficult situations, in decisive challenges or in important decisions. Sensitive people recount how in situations that overwhelmed them, a separation from a partner of many years, or the death of a person close to them, the presence of a dead soul offered great solace: they felt a great strength, and at the same time the dead person was present in their thoughts and feelings. A young woman related that her much-loved, deceased grandmother kept her safe during the many exams she had to take as part of her studies. She was agitated and nervous but the grandmother gave her an assurance and calmness that sustained her. The same woman also said she knew that she had been able to acquire a particular house thanks to her grandmother.

The dead accompany those they have been close to, for many years—really up to the time when these peo- ple themselves die. But the way in which they do so can change over time. If we attend to such things we will be able to observe that the dead gradually enter into a dif- ferent relationship with those they love—they leave them ever freer. At all events they deeply desire that the one they love should take their own life ever more strongly into their own hands. The more they can shape their own des- tiny, the better they can focus on the tasks which the world of spirit entrusts them with.

*

In the life after death the dead remain connected with whatever their love was directed toward. They observe what follows from these loving impulses, how they work on, what direction they take, who takes them up and how they change. They feel deep satisfaction when these loving impulses are taken up by others and led further. During life a person may, for instance, have been dedicated to the idea of organic architecture, undertaking study and research in this domain, perhaps also constructing houses that correspond to their ideas. Then, after death, they will be able to support people who develop similar ideas, even if they never actually met them in life. They can, for instance, act as a kind of patron to an institute that is founded to promote study and teaching of organic architecture. Or they may help individual students of architecture who are interested in this field. An artist after death can support young artists from the world of spirit, and so on. For the dead it signifies great good fortune to be able to continue to oversee the realization of impulses they pursued during life but had to relinquish at death.

21
Soul wounds

We inherit the wounds of our parents and grandparents. The life of our progenitors has a formative effect on us. What they did, omitted to do, what they accomplished and how fulfilled they were, their failings and failures, their disappointments and fears, their despair and their sense of guilt—all this is inscribed in us. Even if they died a long time ago, we are still very close to them. We possess an existential connection with them that survives death; we are in unavoidable conversation with them. At most we can ignore but not deny it. The wounds of our predecessors are always also our own. They pass them on to us in the transformative river of life connecting successive generations with each other. We belong to the living flow of generations by virtue of the fact that those alive on the earth are in conversation with their predecessors. These connections survive so that the transformative work of one generation can pass to the next, for no generation can accomplish its tasks without the help of the succeeding one.

Yet every person has their own wounds: each is always also an injured, chastened child. Wounds and hurts occur continually, an ongoing stream from which the soul receives injury. It is difficult to defend oneself against such injuries: we can overlay them, forget them, conceal them but scarcely prevent them. Hurt happens already because the soul has sympathies, uniting itself far more intensively with what it perceives and experiences than the conscious mind is aware of. A trail of pain remains within it from much that it experiences. The injustices, humiliations, neglect and hatred that lead to such widespread suffering in the world are something we still need to learn not to deny, yet at the same time we must ensure this does not injure our health.

*

Our own wounds are largely invisible, and for good reason. They often lie in regions that can scarcely be noticed. To call them to mind often requires a special skill, a conscious exertion. Or they may suddenly erupt in us involuntarily. Certain circumstances awaken them from their happy-unhappy slumbers. What was forgotten is suddenly summoned and stands there before us. Old things we thought we had freed ourselves from, had dealt with, surface unexpectedly. Forms of behaviour we thought had lost their hold over us suddenly reign supreme again. Fears, anxieties, compulsive inner pictures come to the fore though we hoped we had long since overcome them.

Within us we bear pain, disappointment, injuries, unfulfilled longings and needs that we believe we can only defend ourselves from by forgetting them. Now suppression belongs to life and we cannot exist in this world without recourse to it; yet we can be sure that this is only a short-term solution. Circumstances will arise when what we suppress resurfaces and will demand its dues: to be finally seen, accepted and transformed. Soul wounds break open because it is important for us to engage with them. They bleed again because they heal only when we are fully reconciled with them. But this means that we must learn to really integrate the pain we suffered into our life, our existence, our being. Wounds are a part of our individuality.

They are also always the wellspring of new powers, new inner capacities. There is no wound that cannot become the source of new human potential.

*

Wounds always point to powers of the personality that lie undeveloped within us, which we have not yet realized. To overcome wounds means to push forward into new regions of personal development. This does not at all require us to analyse each and every soul wound in detail. Reconciliation with our own inner wounds does not lie in re-experiencing their pain, but rather in gradually creating new life realities for ourselves. We are by no means simply the passive victims of our destiny. Through inner work we can open up new sources of our personality. There is no compulsion to remain the person we are at present. The soul always has undeveloped regions that require care and cultivation, which we can still school and develop. For instance we can decide to regard life and what it shows us more attentively, to refrain from judgement, to listen more carefully, to respond more positively, to undertake our tasks with more interest, and so on and so forth. All this helps heal the wounds we have, for we are calling upon ourselves to follow new paths, to practise new abilities.

Wounds are painful because they make us aware that our own personality is not perfect, intact or whole but has injuries and defects. The wounds we suffer from show us that we are still on a journey towards the wholeness of our own being.

When a wound that was sunk deep in the soul ocean of forgetting resurfaces and hurts us all over again, this is a sign that it really wishes to be healed. For a while it has lived quietly. When it breaks open again it opens a door that cannot remain shut any longer, for within it our whole and perfect being seeks to become known. It is actually a sacred moment when a wound becomes apparent, for through the veil of frailty strength already shines.

*

We can only be reconciled with things we love. Whatever we reject cannot reveal its true nature. The power of love always underlies the capacity to reconcile oneself to something. To love our own wounds—which we may wish had never happened—is a great and seemingly superhuman step forward. Love, or actually love of ourselves, is the precondition for accepting our hurting, wounded child, the suffering being that each of us bears within. This is a special 'Yes', an affirmation that we only very slowly come to know, perhaps through many incarnations. We are still in the process of trying this out gingerly: perhaps we are only just beginning to think it, and then to utter it ever more loudly.

There is no question that my wounds prevent me from being myself freely, lovingly, calmly and entirely. They weaken me and make of me someone who I am, certainly, with whom I engage intimately day-in, day-out, but who sometimes appears very strange to me. At particular moments we regard ourselves, our carryings-on, and discern the strategies we employ to deceive ourselves and others, and to avoid having to be ourselves entirely. The lies about ourselves we succumb to stand then in clarity before us, and we can hardly find a good word to say about ourselves.

And a seemingly strange thought germinates, though one that gradually gains more and more shape and conviction: *Is it not true, in fact, that I only actually find myself beyond all wounds? Am I not also the person who has no wounds at all?* And then we can ask who this is, this person undamaged and unwounded. What does he look like, where can he be found, and how do we meet him?

I can set out to find this person without wounds. I can attune myself to him and invite him to approach. If we succeed in doing this, we will be surprised to see who it is who appears: a child possessing great power, bearing a light we long for, the light of our own, lofty being.

*

One way to free ourselves from our soul wounds is to become aware of our own potential. If I perceive and value the person I truly am, the painful wounds I suffer because I am grieving, despairing, worn down and humiliated, will pass from me. But this inner being of mine cannot be pressurized, nor commanded. It reveals itself, rather if we practise generosity towards ourselves, if we can shed excessive expectations, when we can look with satisfaction upon what we have already done, and when we succeed in staying tranquil through all the smaller and greater rigours of destiny.

*

Assuredly we are still on the way to becoming true human beings of the earth. We are learning to accept the earth as she shows herself to be at every moment. We are as yet too strange to ourselves, too doubtful and critical of ourselves, to be able to develop the strength to say a wholehearted 'Yes' to our earthly destiny. As yet we respond with great reticence to the love which the earth brings toward us at every moment of our life. To become fully aware of the gifts we receive through living on earth we need a tranquillity of soul that we have to school in ourselves. Stopping to see life, to receive the seemingly infinite life forces of the earth and the cosmos, requires an inner stance that does not arise as a matter of course but only brightens in us through inner work. But the human soul has a strong need to accept the earth. We have a great thirst to connect in depth and fullness with each moment of our lives. We feel dimly how much there is in every moment, more at least than we can grasp at present.

Our 'Yes' to the earth is so hesitant because we sense that uttering it with all our strength would radically transform our life. The earth with her vast, boundless existence would kindle a life in us that we long for but are afraid of too, because it is so big. But we only become ourselves *with* the earth, and the other creatures that live upon her. All that remains for us is to increasingly unite with her, to enhance the powers that will allow us to become one with all living phenomena and beings! Our true potential lies in becoming earthly human beings. The earth is so benevolent that she is still helping us to give birth to ourselves. But this means developing the gesture of complete trust in her, the great mother.

22
Christ in the living earth

Growing awareness of the Christ being is a process whose begin-
nings unfold deep within the soul and therefore often remain
unnoticed. We should not think, therefore, that Christ
reveals himself to us from the outset in the full light of consciousness. In fact, the opposite is true: Christ encompasses
the soul without us necessarily having a clear experience
or idea of what is occurring. This is understandable since
we are, for good reason, entangled in manifold ways in the
events of our earthly life. But this entanglement means that
we cannot always stand in the full truth of our higher life.
Our daily tasks preoccupy us and require our alert attention, and this leads in turn to a dulling of our higher consciousness.

The nature of Christ is that of a being who *is* the light of
truth. For this reason the encounter with Christ challenges
our sense of truthfulness and our truth-seeking. Christ
does not wait for each person to come to the point of standing consciously in the truth of higher life before announcing himself, for he is our teacher in this respect, helping us
grow toward the truth.

The Christ being connects by gradual stages with the
world of earth. We can discern here an evolutionary process in which he only slowly reveals himself to clear human
consciousness. Conscious perception of the Christ being is
therefore preceded by a dreamy, feeling experience of his
presence.

*

Each night during sleep an encounter occurs between the human soul and the Christ being, but without us consciously perceiving this. When the human soul separates from the body, it meets the Christ being in the soul world adjoining the physical world. Christ receives the soul. He takes it up into his world and guides it upon its forthcoming path. This encounter means that Christ endows every human soul with certain virtues or gifts. These are available to us during the day whether or not we make use of them. These gifts which flow toward the human soul through the Christ being make it possible for us to realize impulses intrinsic to us during our life on earth. They serve us as individualities seeking the freedom of our being, enabling us to freely address the tasks of our own destiny. Christ endows human beings with the freedom to choose to follow their destiny or not. He serves the human soul in so far as he endows it with the strength to affirm itself as a being possessing a destiny, yet one that need not be unfree but can fulfil this destiny out of its own free impulses. Christ reveals himself to the conscious human mind only when this gives him cause to. It is up to us to prepare ourselves for this encounter out of our own motivation.

*

Christ wants each individual to acquire the capacity to unite their own destiny with that of humanity and the earth. Each night he quietly prompts us to read the events of our karma as true pictures through which this destiny speaks to us. Destiny itself is the schooling in which each person is taught by Christ. In everything that happens to us we can always also experience the action and influence of the Christ being, since every such occurrence serves us in beholding, respecting and discerning ourselves.

Beholding the events of our life reveals to us the dynamic, powers and themes of the higher self. This higher being is immediately present at every moment of life although it cannot yet be perceived in full clarity. Christ works upon the sleeping soul so that we can be assured of the higher being that is directly active in our destiny and comes to expression there. He helps us to become aware of the power and distinctive nature of our own being, to value and accept it.

*

If we experience the fortunate moment when Christ's nightly gifts to our own being become conscious to us, this is usually associated with a transformation of our previous views and judgements about the nature of life. Henceforth we will know that a lofty being of the world of spirit keeps his protecting hand over us. Likewise we know that nothing at all will be lost of what we do or think, or what we have done and thought. Christ engages in every detail with what issues from us. He examines it and evaluates it from a higher perspective, and he also takes it upon himself. No human deed can be so dire that he declines to take it upon himself. But he also cautions the human soul not to shy away from the responsibility which each person bears, and to accept their shadow as much as their light. Clarity in every respect, in inner observation of ourselves, and in exact observation of what occurs around us, is a quality that he kindles in the human soul.

Christ desires that the need for beings of the world of spirit to intervene in human freedom should continually grow less. Likewise his gifts to us should serve to render us independent of the influences and temptations that seek to divert us from ourselves and our own path.

*

In several lectures given in 1910, Rudolf Steiner described how Christ would appear in the twentieth century in the life of the earth:

> Such changes in human soul capacities will arrive. Something we can term etheric vision will come. And what is associated with this? Well, the being we call the Christ appeared in the flesh at the beginning of the Christian era. He will not come again in this way, in a physical body, for that was a unique event. But in etheric form Christ will return in the times I have referred to. Then, through this etheric vision, human beings will learn to perceive Christ by growing upward toward the one who now no longer descends as far as the physical body but only as far as the etheric body. Thus human beings will need to grow upward toward a perception of the Christ. For what Christ said is true: I am with you always, to the end of all earthly times.[12]

Experiences in this realm are possible if we do not regard the world in exclusively material terms. The spiritual dynamic which the Christ being engenders in the etheric, thus in the very life of the world, is only perceptible to our spiritual senses. This fine, delicate power easily escapes our attention. We can gain experiences of invisible life-streams if we attend empathically to what streams and lives in every plant, every blossom, every creature and every substance. To discern the power which comes from the Christ being and pervades and elevates all living things, we must take inner steps that lead to vision of the life forces of the living ether. Schooling of perception allows us to discern the actions of the Christ being within living reality as an elevating, transforming and nurturing power. Then we feel ourselves beheld by beings within earth's living reality who bear the most sacred powers of transformation.

It is worth pointing out that observation of all cyclical processes in nature is especially helpful in giving us profound and meaningful experiences of the living realm. Even the course of the day offers us many opportunities for this, as do inner observations of what happens over the course of a year in a landscape, in a garden or with a tree. These point us toward an experience of processes that come to expression in the living etheric realm.

*

In the same way we can become attentive to the work of the Christ being in other human beings. But to do so we need to acquire a sense of the uniqueness of the other individuality. The other is always completely different from ourselves, completely distinct from who we are. There are no doubt similarities, affinities and correspondences, but they should not obscure what is meant here. The different nature of another individuality is always compelling and striking. Otherness is intrinsic to the other, and is what makes them our 'opposite number'. The intrinsic uniqueness of each and every person is what makes them our true counterpart.

A person's voice, eyes, movements, the nature of their biography are there to awaken us to the unique qualities of another: they are bridges, doorways, which make it possible to intimate, at least, or sense, the essential being of the other, their high name. As yet the sense realm misleads us so that we perceive another's being only dimly. Really we only dream it. Yet facts and realities impress upon us ever more insistently and unmistakeably what the other person actually is!

In every person Christ lives in his own intrinsic way. For this reason we can perceive him precisely in the other person's individuality. Christ evades all patterns, paradigms, forms, all fixed ideas; or in other words, we cannot grasp him through such patterns, forms and ideas. He can only be experienced beyond the threshold of the world that appears reliable to us. He asks us to develop perceptions of realms of life that do not yet lie within our accustomed notions. He is to be found in left-field glimpses, in stillness; in what only reveals the grandeur of his being by withdrawing and receding. He is present in childlike and natural things, in lightness of being, in the momentary. To discover him in the other person means, in fact, to love the otherness that is all too easily overlooked in the other person. As soon as we succeed—perhaps only with time—in seeing in the other what is only gradually becoming apparent, we behold the activity of the being of the Christ, whose nature it likewise is to conceal his invisible qualities within visible things, since only in this fragile and delicate way can the future reveal itself.

*

We live in a time in which profound, personal and unexpected experiences of Christ are possible. In many lectures Rudolf Steiner speaks of the relationship of modern people to the being of Christ. The following passage is representative of what he says:

> Two aspects of the future are apparent: one is that of aridity, of a succumbing to materialism, but the other

that of the birth of a new world of spirit—not only in our thoughts or, let us say, in our outlooks, but as living reality. Christ will come to stand beside human beings and become their counsellor. This is not meant merely metaphorically but in actual reality, for people will receive the counsels they need from the living Christ, who will be their friend and adviser, and will speak to human souls in the same way as a person who accompanies us physically.[13]

23
The power of forgiveness

After death we experience the consequences of our actions at first hand. It is one of the most surprising insights into the human soul's experiences after death to behold how the being of Christ approaches the one who has died and engages with this soul's culpable actions towards other people and creatures. Christ has a great interest in the culpability with which the human soul enters the world of spirit after death. He turns a deep attentiveness towards this. He helps a person become aware in retrospect of the nature of their culpability. It might be unconsidered or negligent actions, things they did in anger or distress or exhaustion, or malicious actions intended to harm or injure.

Christ shows the dead person the meaning of their actions. And this happens in such a way that the soul experiences the consequences of its actions, both good and bad, as if they were being done to itself. This results in the insight that the bad actions a person has done must *inevitably* be redressed. It becomes clear to us that uncompensated actions cannot exist in the world of spirit, and this gives rise to the absolute desire to make redress for the negative consequences of our own deeds, thus to transform them. From the Christ being there emanates a willingness to accompany the dead person in this process. He shows us that there are instances where we can be relieved of this redress: for instance, it may be that those who have suffered at the hands of the dead person in life have already forgiven them or will do so. If someone affected by a culpable action is already at peace with the perpetrator, the deed has been redressed.

*

In the eyes of Christ, a person's culpability is not something that condemns or brands them but rather something towards which he shows the greatest care and concern. The potential to incur guilt is inevitably connected with a person's stages of individual development. Guilt is the gateway to freedom, but also encompasses the capacity to forgive. Guilt and forgiveness are the source of our transformation into a being who acts with responsibility towards themselves and the world. They are stages that we pass through on our path of development, and without them we do not attain freedom. Christ serves us by supporting us in facing culpability, also our own, out of powers of love. Only through love can real transformation come about.

*

The influence of the being of Christ helps us develop powers of forgiveness. A healing stream issues from the Christ being and seeks to encompass the soul so that it develops the power of forgiveness. The ability to forgive is a gift of Christ to humanity. We can tap into this stream of healing if we resolve to be taught and instructed by Christ. When we desire to be admitted to his school, he will be able to act upon each of us in an intimate and inimitably wondrous way.

Forgiving is a deed that works through into the world of spirit. It does not stop before the gates of heaven but makes available to the spirit beings who govern human destiny a sacred substance of transformation. Through them a spiritual substance is created that works in the whole cosmos with sublime transformative effect.

*

To make redress for personal guilt is not a labour for the person concerned alone. It can also be taken on by others. Ultimately each of us also bears responsibility for the deeds and misdeeds of others since in sleep and after death we come into a state of being in which we are united in soul and spirit with the earth, the cosmos and humanity, as well as with the impulses at work in other people's lives.

In sleep and after death (as well as before birth), each person connects with the culpable actions of human beings. This is all the more so for someone filled with the impulse to transform and heal earthly conditions. Even in sleep they will take up the consequences of transgressions and crimes that have been committed worldwide in the past and are still being committed in the present. We can indeed speak of an unconscious night-work to which the soul devotes itself during sleep. While a person sleeps, the soul substance of love streams out from them and is carried further by spirit beings and used as healing substance. Sleep is a healer not only for each of us individually but also for the whole earth, for through it powers are released that issue from the heart impulses of individual people. A deed that proceeds from loving devotion to a cause or another human being or creature is always a seed that comes to effect in a broader sphere, also permeating sleep and mediated by it.

Supersensible observation shows that many people unconsciously and yet tirelessly work to resolve what has been engendered by culpable conduct on the earth in the past, and in the present. Guilt cannot be redressed in the world of spirit but only by impulses of love that ripen on earth. Guilt arises on earth and only there can it be resolved by powers that proceed from the processes of development and maturation of individual people. Forgiveness is a power which, though founded on individual impulse, is intrinsically transpersonal. It has an effect that radiates outward, far beyond the single individual. This is why it works further in sleep and after death as a healing substance within the entirety of the cosmos.

*

When someone commits a crime that burdens them with great guilt, through an attack that ends the lives of many others, and their own, very suddenly and unexpectedly, it can be observed among other things that those whose death this person caused gather around him in the life after death. Those who were killed concern themselves with his welfare. He stands at the centre of a group of people whom he killed. In a single moment a destiny community is created by this inconceivable action between people who may not have previously known each other. At some point the perpetrator becomes aware of what he has done: he perceives the consequences of his action and has a deep need for remorse and repentance. He has committed the crime in a state in which he was not himself. In the after-death realm he feels the compulsion that was practised upon him and misled him to take this action. He experiences how he was no more than a will-less victim whose true feeling for human qualities has been eradicated. He feels that he both committed and did not commit this crime. He would do all in his power to undo it but cannot do so. And now it is astonishing and moving to observe him being comforted by some of those who, at odds with their own destiny, have passed with him into the world of spirit. They share in his torments! Not all of them are able to do this, but some can look from the spiritual world upon his deed and experience its deeper cause. Due to the terribly sudden and untimely change in their condition they may still be in shock and not even be fully aware of what has actually happened to them, but this does not prevent them from turning to the one among them who is compelled to suffer the greatest torments. The victims comfort the perpetrator, who is himself a victim. They comfort the one who, swiftly after his deed, is shown its consequences by Christ. It is fully in accord with the nature of Christ that the victims help the perpetrator to alleviate his almost unbearable anguish. They urge him to take heart. They may not even realize yet that they have been murdered by him, but they offer him solace because this is essential.

*

If you immerse yourself in the earth's spiritual nature, you can discover that a vessel lies within it which contains a fluid substance composed of the pain you have both suffered and inflicted. Everything you have ever suffered as well as the suffering you have culpably inflicted upon other beings is present in this vessel. From within the earth this is handed to you, rising toward you so that you can receive it. We must not reject it for it belongs to us. Guilt is a part of our individuality, as also are the humiliations and pain we have suffered. They have inscribed themselves in our soul through the life it has led on earth. Reconciliation and atonement are accomplished when we accept this vessel extended to us, when we take hold of it and raise it upwards. No more than this is needed. Atonement is not something that should exceed our own powers for otherwise it could not be accomplished. It must always correspond to the strength we possess. If we do not manage to accept this vessel in its entirety then we first turn to smaller quotas. In this way we progress to the point where we can raise the whole vessel.

*

Each of us is the bearer of a transforming and healing substance, whose quality depends on our own development. This substance can remain very hidden in our actual life but it is nevertheless very much at work in the background, and can be discerned by empathic perception. We can meet people whose life does not at first glance seem to show that they have a spiritual substance of great goodness to impart. But if we look more carefully at what emanates from them, it becomes apparent that the mission they are pursuing in this life does not necessarily allow the healing and transforming powers they have already attained to become apparent. We need only develop the right way of seeing, one that is not deceived by appearance but turns to the other's supersensible characteristics. A person's higher nature shines continually. It is superficial to judge someone only according to what is immediately apparent in them, for we can never do someone justice in this way. We have to seek a different standpoint, another perspective if we wish to recognize the other's true qualities.

In particular, people who remain dependent on others, caring for them throughout their lives, sometimes have a very potent spiritual emanation that reaches into the elemental world, and there ensures that the elemental beings can orient themselves—something like a spiritual luminosity. In children, too, we can often perceive that they bear a higher light, which is imbibed by the beings of the elemental world because they no longer receive it from older, adult people. Natural religiosity, attentiveness, care, esteem and respect provide tangible help for the earth and the beings connected with her, since they originate in what people have already achieved by way of powers of transformation from former lives, or else that have become available to them naturally in this life. Impulses of transformation issue from people who by no means always perceive this themselves. We are only slowly acquiring concepts for this.

*

Forgiving is a significant deed. To find the strength to forgive the person who has mistreated or harmed us, but also to forgive oneself for the actions which did harm, are important steps in human development. Forgiveness means dissolving existing shadows and hindrances. This endows us with the ability to heal troublesome social conditions. From this perspective, forgiveness is a healing social deed. It unburdens and liberates social conditions so often burdened by the consequences of culpable conduct.

*

For the soul who is not yet born the earth is a second heaven. Deep, deep is the desire to leave nothing out that can be experienced upon earth. This strength of union with the earth, this ability to become a part of her being, to merge with her, is at the same time the power enabling us to shape ourselves in an upright human body. In the human soul lives the wish to belong utterly to the earth. The longing for earthly experiences burns within the soul; it seeks to absorb what can be absorbed; it seeks to learn what can only be learned upon earth. The love-imbued wish to belong to the earth, to fuse and become one with her, is the power that enables the soul to overcome the heaviness and the sluggishness of the body. *The gift that underlies lightness and uprightness is love, and upon this is founded the power of forgiveness.*

Afterword

This book rounds off the circle that began seven years ago with *School of the Elemental Beings*. That first book, and the subsequent four (except for *Die Wolkenschrift*—'Script of the Clouds') are really one. I wish to thank [my German-language publisher] Futurum Verlag for publishing these books, especially Claudia Zangger and Jonathan Stauffer, but also editors Taja Gut, Nana Badenberg and Andreas Laudert, who offered me a great deal of support. Finally I want to give my warm thanks to Franziska van der Geest who designed the cover pictures of the first three books [in German].

Notes

1. Goethe, *Maximen und Reflexionen* ('Maxims and Reflections'), Munich 2006.
2. James Stephens, *The Boyhood of Fionn*. Quoted from www.sacred-texts.com.
3. John O'Donohue, *Anam Cara, Spiritual Wisdom from the Celtic World*, Transworld 2011, pp. 98-9.
4. Mircea Eliade, *Shamanism: Archaic Techniques of Ecstasy*, Princeton University Press 2020, p. 98.
5. Hans Findeisen/Heino Gehrts, *Die Schamanen*, Munich 1993, p. 32f.
6. *The Kalevala*, Penguin 2021.
7. Alexandra Morton, *Listening to Whales, What the Orcas Have Taught Us*, Random House 2004, pp. 113-15.
8. In Helmut Schreier, *Bäume. Streifzüge durch eine unbekannte Welt*, p. 255f., Hamburg 2004.
9. Stylianos Atteshlis (Daskalos), *Esoterische Lehren*, Nicosia 2015.
10. John O'Donohue, *Anam Cara*, Bantam Books 1999, p. 99.
11. Op. cit., p. 57.
12. Rudolf Steiner, *The Reappearance of Christ in the Etheric*, GA 118, Anthroposophic Press 1983.
13. Rudolf Steiner, *Approaching the Mystery of Golgotha*, GA 152, Temple Lodge 2005.

A note from the publisher

For more than a quarter of a century, **Temple Lodge Publishing** has made available new thought, ideas and research in the field of spiritual science.

Anthroposophy, as founded by Rudolf Steiner (1861-1925), is commonly known today through its practical applications, principally in education (Steiner-Waldorf schools) and agriculture (biodynamic food and wine). But behind this outer activity stands the core discipline of spiritual science, which continues to be developed and updated. True science can never be static and anthroposophy is living knowledge.

Our list features some of the best contemporary spiritual-scientific work available today, as well as introductory titles. So, visit us online at **www.templelodge.com** and join our emailing list for news on new titles.

If you feel like supporting our work, you can do so by buying our books or making a direct donation (we are a non-profit/charitable organisation).

office@templelodge.com

☀ TEMPLE LODGE

For the finest books of Science and Spirit